COOK ISLANDS TRAVl

Discover the Secrets of the Cook Islands: Your
Essential Travel Companion for an
Unforgettable Journey With Perfect Itinerary
for First Timers.

Patsy J. Tour

Patsy J. Tour

COOK ISLANDS
Travel Guide 2023

Discover the Secrets of the Cook Islands: Your Essential Travel Companion for an Unforgettable Journey with Perfect Itinerary for First Timers.

TABLE OF CONTENTS

INTRODUCTION.

On a chilly winter day, I came upon a beautiful snapshot of pristine beaches and crystal-clear turquoise seas. The picture drew me in, speaking of tropical happiness and adventure. I was intrigued to learn that this exquisite paradise was none other than the Cook Islands, a hidden jewel in the center of the Pacific Ocean.

I set off for Rarotonga, the biggest of the Cook Islands, with visions of bright sunlight and calm ocean breezes. When I stepped off the aircraft, I was welcomed with a kind warmth that quickly surrounded me. The island greeted me warmly, and I easily adjusted into its routine. I was charmed by the island's natural splendor from the minute I arrived. I set out on a trekking adventure to Te Rua Manga, sometimes known locally as "The Needle." The brilliant colors and unique bird sounds surrounding me as I strolled through lush jungles, offering an immersive experience that stirred my soul.

Dive into the stunning underwater environment of the Cook Islands was a life-changing event. With snorkeling equipment in hand, I discovered an underwater rainbow of coral gardens alive with colourful marine life. Swimming with colorful fish, beautiful turtles, and even playful dolphins, I felt a deep connection to the grandeur of the ocean.

Eager to learn more, I traveled to Aitutaki, a postcard-perfect paradise. I floated over transparent seas on a lagoon tour, past gorgeous motus (small islands) ornamented with waving palm palms. My journey's highlight was arriving to One Foot Island, where I wandered down the powdered white beach, feeling the warm embrace of the sun and the soft lapping of waves at my feet.

I immersed myself in the Cook Islands' unique Polynesian culture to properly comprehend it. I saw a captivating dance performance in which beautiful movements portrayed the story of ancient legends and customs. When I interacted with the people, I noticed their genuine friendliness and strong pride in their history. My cultural experience was further enhanced by learning the craft of traditional weaving and relishing in exquisite island food. As my stay in the Cook Islands came to an end, I was overcome with a bittersweet sense. The experiences I had created, the friendships I had formed, and the pure beauty of the islands would live on in my heart forever. I say goodbye to this paradise with a sad heart, knowing that a piece of it would always be a part of me.

Years have gone since my unforgettable trip to the Cook Islands, but the attraction and enchantment of those days remain with me. My wanderlust is fueled by the vibrant sunsets, the rhythmic rhythms of island music, and the real kindness of the people. The

Cook Islands gave me a chapter of my life that I will remember forever—an exquisite story of chance and finding paradise.

CHAPTER 1: Welcome to Cook Islands.

The Cook Islands are a beautiful archipelago of 15 islands located in the center of the South Pacific Ocean. This self-governing territory in free association with New Zealand has stunning beaches, clean lagoons, and a lively Polynesian culture that draws people from all over the world.

The Cook Islands are separated into two groups geographically: the Northern Group and the Southern Group. Manihiki, Rakahanga, Penrhyn, Pukapuka, Nassau, and Suwarrow are the six distant atolls that make up the Northern Group. These remote atolls are noted for their untouched natural beauty and provide a feeling of tranquillity and isolation.

Rarotonga, Aitutaki, Mangaia, Atiu, Mauke, Mitiaro, Manuae, Palmerston, and Takutea comprise the Southern Group, which is the more populated and popular of the two. Rarotonga, the biggest and most developed island, serves as the Cook Islands' administrative and cultural center. Its high mountain peaks, green jungles, and breathtaking shoreline make it an enticing destination for nature lovers and adventurers alike.

The Cook Islands are a patchwork of gorgeous beaches, with lengths of white sand kissed by blue Pacific seas. Aitutaki is sometimes regarded as a heaven inside a paradise because of its magnificent lagoon. The clear waters are teeming with marine life, allowing snorkelers and divers to explore vivid coral gardens and swim alongside tropical fish and beautiful turtles.

The Cook Islands are filled with a vibrant Polynesian culture that captivates visitors in addition to their picture-perfect surroundings. The friendliness and kindness of the Cook Island Maori people make tourists feel welcome. Traditional arts and crafts, including as delicate weaving and carving, are shown in local markets and galleries, offering insights into the skilled handiwork of the islanders.

Music and dance are essential components of the Cook Islands' cultural character. Traditional performances use throbbing drum rhythms, rhythmic motions, and bright costumes to tell tales about old traditions and rituals. Visitors may experience these enthralling cultural exhibits during festivals and events such as the Te Maeva Nui Festival, which commemorates the Cook Islands' independence and features traditional music, dance, and sports.

The tourist sector is important to the Cook Islands' economy. The natural beauty of the islands, along with their inviting environment, draws people looking for a quiet getaway. Luxury resorts and boutique hotels, as well as guesthouses and self-catering lodgings, cater to a wide variety of interests. With its combination of Pacific tastes, local food tantalizes taste buds and provides a great gourmet experience.

Outdoor enthusiasts will find a wide range of things to enjoy, from swimming and sunbathing on lovely beaches to hiking paths that weave through tropical rainforests. Water activities like as kayaking, paddleboarding, and sailing are available for thrill seekers, as are fishing expeditions to catch the Pacific's bounty.

The Cook Islands prioritize environmental protection and sustainable tourism. With the construction of marine reserves and conservation programs, efforts are undertaken to safeguard and maintain the sensitive marine ecosystems. During their stay, visitors are urged to appreciate the natural environment and partake in eco-friendly behaviors.

The Cook Islands are easy to visit, with daily flights linking the islands to a variety of worldwide places. Rarotonga International Airport serves as the Cook Islands' international gateway, receiving flights from New Zealand, Australia, and other Pacific island nations.

Finally, the Cook Islands provide an enthralling combination of natural beauty, colorful culture, and genuine hospitality. A trip to the Cook Islands promises a unique experience that will leave an everlasting stamp on the soul, whether it's sunbathing on beautiful beaches, immersing oneself in ancient practices, or experiencing the marvels of the undersea world.

Background History of Cook Islands

The Cook Islands, a self-governing territory in the South Pacific, have a long and complicated history stretching back thousands of years. The following is a short history of the Cook Islands:

Polynesians initially established the Cook Islands circa 1500 BC, arriving in canoes from other regions of Polynesia.

These early inhabitants carried their language, culture, and customs with them, which have helped create the Cook Islands' identity to this day. The Cook Islands were discovered by European explorers in the late 18th century. The British sailor Captain James Cook, who arrived in 1773 and named the archipelago after himself, was the first European to see the islands. In the nineteenth century, merchants, missionaries, and whalers visited the islands, continuing European interaction and exploration.

Christian missionaries came in the Cook Islands in the early nineteenth century, bringing with them new religious ideas and Western influences.

The introduction of missionaries had a huge influence on Cook Islands culture and civilization, leading to the conversion of many islanders to Christianity and the building of Christian churches that are still prominent today.

The Cook Islands became a British protectorate, controlled by New Zealand, in 1888. This agreement provided the islands with stability and safety while providing New Zealand great control over their government. The Cook Islands were administered by New Zealand until 1965, when they became self-governing in free association with New Zealand.

Political Development and Self-Government:

The Cook Islands became a self-governing territory with free association with New Zealand in 1965. The Cook Islands have autonomy in most internal issues, but depend on New Zealand for military and international affairs.

The Cook Islands have created their own parliamentary system and have had a series of democratically elected administrations throughout the years.

The Cook Islands have worked hard to preserve and promote their distinct Polynesian culture. The local community values and celebrates cultural traditions such as dance, music, crafts, and language.

Tourism is important to the Cook Islands' economy because tourists are attracted to the islands' natural beauty, clean beaches, and great friendliness. Today, the Cook Islands remain a dynamic and culturally diverse destination. The Cook Islands embrace their Polynesian history while adjusting to the contemporary world's difficulties and possibilities.

Customs and Culture

The Cook Islands' culture and customs are strongly steeped in Polynesian traditions, reflecting the people' profound connection to their land, history, and way of life. Here is an outline of Cook Islands culture and customs:

The Cook Islands' culture is mostly Maori, and Maori is commonly spoken. Maori rituals, arts, and oral traditions are vital to the identity of the islanders. Respect, hospitality, and community are traditional Maori values that are highly valued and serve as the foundation for social relationships.

Dance, music, and drumming are vivid and dynamic forms of creative expression in the Cook Islands. The most well-known traditional dance is the "hula," which is distinguished by rhythmic hip motions, hand gestures, and colorful attire.

Drums, ukuleles, and stringed instruments such as the guitar, as well as the distinctive Cook Islands drum known as the pate, are examples of traditional musical instruments.

Tivaevae is a traditional Cook Islands craft that involves making intricately patterned quilts. Tivaevae making is a social activity in which women meet to sew and tell tales, and the resulting quilts are culturally and artistically significant. Tapu is a cultural idea that is very prominent in the Cook Islands. It alludes to anything holy, forbidden, or limited. Certain locations, items, or behaviors may be deemed tapu and must be treated with respect and avoided. To demonstrate cultural sensitivity, it is critical to accept local advice and observe tapu.

The Cook Islands put a high value on family and community ties. Extended family networks, called as "kainga," are very important in social and cultural life.

Elder respect and communal collaboration are highly prized, and there is a strong feeling of joint responsibility for the community's well-being.

The availability of native resources, as well as the influence of Polynesian and European culinary traditions, are reflected in Cook Islands cuisine. Ika mata (raw fish marinated in lime and coconut), rukau (taro leaves cooked with coconut cream), and umu (traditional subterranean oven cooking) are also popular meals.

The Cook Islands also have a culture of eating and commemorating significant occasions with ceremonies such as "umu ti," in which food is cooked in an underground oven.

The Cook Islands' major religion is Christianity, primarily Protestantism. Churches have an important role in society, and religious observances and festivals are major cultural events.

Festivals of Culture:

Throughout the year, the Cook Islands organize a variety of cultural events that showcase native music, dancing, crafts, and food. Te Maeva Nui, celebrated annually in July, celebrates the islands' self-government while also presenting traditional performances.

When visiting the Cook Islands, it is essential to respect and accept the local traditions and cultural practices. Learning a few words in Maori, engaging in cultural events, and being attentive of local customs can improve your trip and demonstrate respect for the Cook Islands' rich cultural legacy.

21 Reasons You Should Visit Cook Islands

With their natural beauty and rich Polynesian culture, the Cook Islands provide a wealth of compelling reasons to visit. From magnificent vistas to friendly hospitality, the islands offer visitors a one-of-a-kind and memorable experience. Here are 21 compelling reasons why you should visit the Cook Islands:

> ➢ Beautiful Beaches: The Cook Islands have some of the most beautiful beaches in the world, with fluffy white sands and turquoise seas that encourage you to rest and unwind.
>
> ➢ The transparent lagoons that surround the islands provide wonderful chances for snorkeling, swimming, and exploring vivid coral gardens.
>
> ➢ Aitutaki Lagoon: A real tropical paradise, Aitutaki's fabled lagoon is recognized for its spectacular beauty and romantic mood.
>
> ➢ Explore Rarotonga's stunning rainforests, where luscious vegetation, magnificent mountains, and flowing waterfalls make an exquisite environment for trekking and nature tours.

- Te Rua Manga (The Needle): For panoramic views of the island and its surroundings, go to the top of Te Rua Manga, a remarkable needle-like hill in Rarotonga.
- Polynesian Culture: Immerse yourself in the Cook Islands' rich Polynesian culture, complete with vivid music, traditional dance performances, and welcoming hospitality.
- Te Maeva Nui Festival: The Te Maeva Nui Festival is a spectacular celebration of the Cook Islands' freedom that includes traditional singing, dancing, sports, and cultural exhibits.
- Discover the complex art of Cook Islands handicrafts including weaving, carving, and tivaevae (quilting), which exhibit the islanders' extraordinary skill.
- Island hopping: Visit the Cook Islands' several islands, each with its own distinct appeal, from the busy bustle of Rarotonga to the tranquil serenity of the distant atolls.
- Spectacular Sunsets: Behold stunning sunsets that paint the sky with bright colours, providing a captivating background for romantic nights.
- Locals are noted for their warm hospitality and friendly manner, making tourists feel like they are a part of the community.
- Delicious Cook Islands Cuisine: Savor the tastes of the Pacific with fresh seafood, tropical fruits, and distinctive

meals like ika mata (marinated raw fish) and rukau (cooked taro leaves).

- ➢ Relaxation in an Island Setting: Embrace the laid-back island lifestyle and unwind in the quiet surroundings, where time appears to slow down, enabling you to recuperate and discover inner peace.
- ➢ Water Sports: Take advantage of the crystal-clear seas and mild ocean currents by participating in exhilarating water sports such as kayaking, paddleboarding, jet skiing, and sailing.
- ➢ Cultural Villages: Visit traditional villages to obtain insight into the Cook Islanders' daily lives and traditions, gaining a greater knowledge of their culture and history.
- ➢ Hiking & Nature Trails: Take picturesque walks and nature trails through lush woods, secluded valleys, and panoramic overlooks with spectacular views of the islands.
- ➢ Fishing Expeditions: Go on a fishing adventure and try your hand at deep-sea angling for valued catches like marlin, tuna, and mahi-mahi.
- ➢ Romantic Getaways: The Cook Islands provide the ideal setting for a romantic getaway, with quiet beaches,

luxurious resorts, and intimate dining experiences that leave couples with wonderful memories.

➢ Wellness & Spa Retreats: In a calm tropical location, pamper yourself with revitalizing spa treatments, yoga sessions, and wellness retreats that feed both the body and spirit.

➢ Cultural Workshops: Attend cultural workshops to learn traditional crafts, dancing, food, or language, and obtain a better understanding of the Cook Islands' cultural legacy.

➢ Scenic Flights: Take a scenic flight and marvel at the breathtaking aerial views of the islands, coral reefs, and the great Pacific Ocean.

These 21 reasons showcase the Cook Islands' attractiveness and enchantment, luring visitors with their natural beauty, cultural diversity, and opportunity for leisure, exploration, and unique encounters.

Important Things you must know Before Visiting the Cook Islands.

Before traveling to the Cook Islands, it is essential to educate oneself with key things to guarantee a pleasant and memorable vacation. From travel regulations to cultural customs, here are a few things you should know before visiting the Cook Islands:

> ➢ Geographically, the Cook Islands are located in the South Pacific Ocean, northeast of New Zealand. It is essential to have a fundamental awareness of the geography of the islands, including their layout, principal islands, and distance from other attractions.

> ➢ Check the Cook Islands' admission requirements before traveling. Most travelers will need a passport that is valid for at least six months. Some nationalities may need a visa, while others may be able to enter without one.

> ➢ The Cook Islands' official currency is the New Zealand dollar (NZD). Check the current exchange rates and make sure you have enough cash or credit cards acceptable on the islands.

> ➢ Cook Islands Maori and English are the official languages of the Cook Islands. While English is commonly spoken,

learning a few basic Maori words helps improve relationships with natives and demonstrate respect for their culture.

➢ Climate and Weather: The Cook Islands enjoy a tropical climate with warm temperatures all year. During the rainy season, from November to March, expect humid weather, intermittent rainfall, and the possibility of cyclones.

➢ Pack Lightweight, breathable clothes appropriate for warm weather. Remember to bring sunscreen, hats, sunglasses, bug repellent, and appropriate walking shoes. Include swimsuit and snorkeling equipment if you want to participate in water sports.

➢ Time Zone: The Cook Islands use Cook Island Standard Time (GMT-10), which may vary from the time zone in your native country. Make the necessary changes to ensure that your travel preparations and schedule go well.

➢ Health and security: Make sure you have enough travel insurance to handle any medical emergency. Before flying, it is best to visit your healthcare professional about the essential vaccines and prescriptions.

➢ Respect for local traditions and etiquette is crucial in the Cook Islands. Learn about cultural standards such as removing your shoes while visiting houses and religious locations. It is polite to greet strangers with a cordial "kia ora" (hello).

- Conservation & Environmental Responsibility: The Cook Islands put a high value on environmental protection. Learn about conservation initiatives and eco-friendly behaviors including limiting plastic waste and avoiding hurting coral reefs.

- Transport & Getting Around: The main island of Rarotonga has a steady bus service that circles the island. Taxis and automobile rental services are also available. Transportation choices on neighboring islands may be restricted, so plan accordingly.

- Wi-Fi and communication: Wi-Fi is available in most hotels, cafés, and public spaces, however connection speeds may vary. Consider obtaining a local SIM card for data or exploring your service provider's foreign roaming alternatives.

- Electricity: The Cook Islands employ 240V electrical systems with plugs similar to those used in Australia and New Zealand. If your gadgets have various plug types, bring adapters.

- Shopping and Dining: Shop for original Cook Islands handicrafts, pearls, and local vegetables to support local businesses. Taste traditional cuisine and fresh fish at the island's restaurants.

- ➢ Respect the Land and People: The Cook Islands have a close relationship with their land and customs. Respect holy places, private property, and the way of life in the area. Before photographing anyone, get their permission.
- ➢ Weather-Related Preparation: Be prepared for flight interruptions or itinerary adjustments due to cyclones or extreme weather conditions during the rainy season. Keep up with weather updates and obey local authorities' directions.
- ➢ Banking services and ATMs are accessible on Rarotonga and Avarua, but may be restricted on other islands. To avoid card limits, prepare your cash requirements carefully and tell your bank of your vacation intentions.
- ➢ Local Events and Festivals: Consult the calendar to see what cultural events and festivals are taking place during your stay. Attending these festivals offers a once-in-a-lifetime chance to witness traditional music, dancing, and rituals.
- ➢ Island Time: The Cook Islands have a leisurely and easygoing pace known as "Island Time." Embrace this laid-back attitude, be patient, and appreciate the slower rhythms of island life.

- ➤ Environmental Considerations: By practicing responsible tourism, you can help maintain the Cook Islands' delicate ecosystems. To preserve the underwater ecosystem, avoid touching or treading on coral reefs and obey marine activity restrictions.
- ➤ Embrace the Spirit of Aloha: Above all, embrace the Cook Islanders' warm welcome and genuine kindness. Immerse yourself in their culture, make friends with the people, and leave lasting impressions via meaningful encounters.
- ➤ By being acquainted with these important details, you may assure an enjoyable and courteous vacation to the picturesque Cook Islands. In this tropical paradise, enjoy the natural beauty, embrace the culture, and create amazing experiences.

The Dos and Don'ts in the Cook Islands

When visiting the Cook Islands, it is essential to be informed of local traditions and practices in order to respect the culture and have a great experience. Understanding the dos and don'ts will help you explore the islands and communicate appropriately with the inhabitants.

Dos:

- As a demonstration of respect and kindness, greet locals with a smile and a pleasant "kia ora" (hello).
- It is usual to remove your shoes before entering houses, traditional gathering places (marae), and certain businesses.
- Ask for permission before photographing people, particularly in more personal or holy circumstances.
- Respect the local traditions and customs. Learn about the culture and participate in activities that reflect respect and gratitude.
- Shop for genuine Cook Islands handicrafts, pearls, and locally created goods to support local companies.
- Do engage in responsible tourism and environmentally good practices, such as reducing plastic trash and avoiding damaging coral reefs.
- To respect local traditions, dress modestly while visiting villages, religious places, or cultural activities.
- To immerse yourself in the local culture, visit the islands and participate in cultural activities such as traditional dance, weaving, or culinary workshops.

- To sample the flavors of the Cook Islands, enjoy indigenous food such as ika mata (marinated raw fish) and rukau (cooked taro leaves).
- Take care of the natural environment and be aware of your surroundings. To safeguard sensitive ecosystems, stick to established routes and follow directions.

Don'ts:

- When visiting communities, religious places, or cultural activities, avoid wearing exposing or improper clothing. Dress modestly and observe local traditions.
- While snorkeling or participating in aquatic sports, do not touch or foot on coral reefs. By appreciating from a distance, you may help conserve the fragile marine habitat.
- Do not litter or leave rubbish. Keep the islands clean and attractive by properly disposing of your rubbish.
- Don't offend or dismiss the local culture, traditions, or beliefs. Show respect and understanding for the Cook Islands' customs.
- Swimming or entering restricted regions without permission is not permitted, since certain spots may have cultural or spiritual value to the residents.

➤ Take no shells, corals, or other natural treasures from beaches or sea areas. To preserve the ecological balance, leave them as you found them.

➤ Don't be impatient or hurried. Accept the relaxed "Island Time" attitude and appreciate the slower pace of life in the Cook Islands.

➤ When purchasing, avoid haggling excessively. While some bargaining may be allowed in local marketplaces, remember to be courteous and consider reasonable rates for products and services.

➤ Respect holy areas, such as marae (traditional gathering places) or burial grounds. Pay attention to any warnings or instructions about access and conduct.

➤ Feeding or stroking animals is an example of an activity that may damage wildlife or disturb natural ecosystems.

You may show respect for the local culture, contribute positively to the community, and have a satisfying stay in the Cook Islands by following these dos and don'ts. In this Polynesian paradise, embrace the traditions, immerse yourself in the natural beauty, and make unforgettable experiences.

Making Travel Plans

A journey to the Cook Islands requires some key actions to guarantee a pleasant and pleasurable experience. When arranging your vacation, keep the following points in mind:

Choose the Best Time to Visit:

The Cook Islands have a tropical environment with mild temperatures all year. The dry season, from May to October, is the busiest for tourists since the weather is normally good and rainfall is limited. When deciding when to go, consider your preferences for weather, people, and pricing.

Make a Budget:

Make a budget for your vacation, taking into consideration lodging, transportation, food, activities, and any other costs.

Compare rates for flights, lodging (hotels, resorts, guesthouses, or vacation rentals), and activities to verify they are within your budget.

Make an itinerary:

Determine the length of your stay and plan your schedule around your interests and priorities. Consider the islands you want to visit as well as the activities you want to participate in.

The Cook Islands are made up of 15 major islands, the most popular and readily accessible of which is Rarotonga. Consider visiting Aitutaki, which is noted for its beautiful lagoon, as well as other islands for a more diversified experience.

Book your flights and lodging:

Look for flights to Rarotonga International Airport (RAR), the Cook Islands' primary gateway. Compare rates and book your flights early to get the best offers.

Early planning and booking of accommodations ensures availability and secures your desired location and style of accommodation.

Examine the Passport and Visa Requirements:

Check that your passport is valid for at least six months after your intended travel date. Check the visa requirements for your nationality by visiting the Cook Islands Immigration Department's official website or contacting the closest Cook Islands embassy or consulate.

Pack as follows:

Pack lightweight and breathable clothes, swimsuits, sunscreen, hats, and sunglasses suited for the tropical temperature.

Don't forget travel adapters, bug repellant, and other prescriptions you may need.

Excursions and research activities:

Investigate the activities and attractions you wish to see and do in the Cook Islands. Snorkeling, diving, lagoon cruises, hiking, cultural excursions, and attending local markets and festivals are all possibilities.

To ensure your space, book or reserve popular activities in advance, particularly during high seasons.

Travel Protection:

Consider obtaining travel insurance to cover medical costs, trip cancellations, and lost or stolen items. Check that your insurance policy covers any particular activities you want to participate in, such as water sports or adventure activities.

Discover Local Customs & Etiquette:

Familiarize oneself with the Cook Islands' customs, traditions, and manners. When engaging with locals, respect the local culture and be cognizant of proper conduct, clothing regulations, and traditions.

Keep Up to Date:

Keep up to current on Cook Islands travel warnings, weather conditions, and any special needs or rules. For the most up-to-date information, visit the Cook Islands Tourism Corporation's official website and check with reliable sources.

By properly arranging your vacation to the Cook Islands, you can make the most of your time there and create long-lasting memories.

When Is the Best Time to Visit?

The Cook Islands have a nice tropical temperature all year, but the ideal time to visit depends on your weather, activity interests, and crowd levels. Here are some things to think about when deciding whether to visit the Cook Islands:

During the dry season (May to October)

In the Cook Islands, the dry season is considered the main tourism season, with typically good weather and little rainfall.

Temperatures vary from 20°C (68°F) to 26°C (79°F) over this time period, making it ideal for outdoor activities.

The dry season is excellent for beach activities, snorkeling, diving, and experiencing the natural beauty of the islands.

Season for Whale Watching (July to October):

If you want to go whale watching, the months of July through October are optimal. During this season, humpback whales pass through the Cook Islands, and there are scheduled cruises available to see these amazing animals.

During the wet season (November to April),

The Cook Islands' rainy season is distinguished by greater temperatures and heavier rainfall. Even at this time of year, rain showers are typically brief, and the islands remain lush and verdant.

For those seeking for reduced pricing, fewer people, and a more relaxed environment, the rainy season might be an excellent time to come. Photographers may also take advantage of the brilliant hues and lush sceneries.

Season of Cyclones (November to April):

During the rainy season, especially from January to March, the Cook Islands are vulnerable to cyclones (tropical storms). While cyclones are uncommon, it is important to keep updated about meteorological conditions and to heed any instructions or warnings provided by local authorities.

Festivals and events:

Consider the dates of any unique events or festivals you want to attend. Throughout the year, the Cook Islands organize a variety of cultural festivals, such as Te Maeva Nui (July), which commemorates the islands' self-government and includes traditional performances and cultural exhibits.

The ideal time to visit the Cook Islands is determined by your own tastes. The dry season, which runs from May through October, is suggested if you want bright and dry weather with a lively environment. However, if you don't mind a few raindrops, want to avoid crowds, and want to pay less, the rainy season from November to April may be a decent alternative.

Length of Stay

The length of your stay in the Cook Islands is determined by your travel choices, the activities you want to participate in, and the islands you want to see. Here are some things to think about while deciding how long to stay:

Exploration of the Main Island:

If you wish to spend most of your time on the main island of Rarotonga, allow at least 3 to 5 days to enjoy its gorgeous beaches, hiking trails, cultural attractions, and local markets.

This time range enables you to see the island's attractions, such as cultural events at Te Vara Nui Village, touring Muri Lagoon, and having a picturesque drive across the island's coastline route.

Island hopping and long stays:

If you want to visit various islands in the Cook Islands, such as Rarotonga, Aitutaki, and Atiu, you should consider staying for a longer period of time.

A suggested stay of 7 to 10 days or more allows time to travel between islands, immerse yourself in the distinct offers of each island, and participate in activities including as snorkeling, diving, and cultural excursions.

Beach Time and Relaxation:

A minimum stay of 5 to 7 days is recommended if your main purpose is to unwind, relax on beautiful beaches, and absorb in the natural beauty of the Cook Islands.

This time frame enables you to enjoy lazy beach days, water activities, and the peacefulness of the islands at your own pace.

Festivals or Special Events:

Consider the length of the event and add a few additional days to explore the region outside of the celebrations if you want to attend certain events or festivals in the Cook Islands.

For example, if you want to experience Te Maeva Nui, the Cook Islands' self-governance festival celebrated in July, you should plan on spending at least a week immersing yourself in cultural events and seeing the islands.

Personal Preferences and Interests:

Consider the activities and experiences you want to have during your visit. If you have certain hobbies, such as scuba diving, trekking, or cultural immersion, you may wish to prolong your stay to fully participate in these activities.

Remember that the Cook Islands have a relaxed and tranquil attitude, so making time to relax and appreciate the natural surroundings is key. Whether you visit for a short or long period of time, the Cook Islands will give you with a wonderful and revitalizing experience.

How to Get to the Cook Islands

Getting to the Cook Islands is mostly done by plane. When planning a trip to the Cook Islands, keep the following points in mind:

Flights to other countries:

Rarotonga International Airport (RAR) serves as the Cook Islands' primary international gateway. Several airlines fly to Rarotonga from diverse locations including of New Zealand, Australia, Fiji, Tahiti, and Los Angeles.

You may need to schedule a connecting flight to one of these transit hubs before boarding a trip to Rarotonga, depending on your location.

Time of flight:

The flight time to the Cook Islands varies based on your departure location. Flights from Auckland, New Zealand, take 3-4 hours, whereas flights from Sydney, Australia, take 6 hours.

Expect a lengthier trip time if you are flying from North America, which normally ranges from 10 to 12 hours depending on the route and any layovers.

Airlines:

Air New Zealand is the primary airline that offers direct flights from Auckland, New Zealand to Rarotonga. They also provide connections from other foreign places.

Other airlines, like Virgin Australia, Jetstar, and Air Tahiti, provide stopovers at their respective hubs.

Requirements for Admission:

Make sure you have a passport that is valid for at least six months beyond your scheduled travel date.

Check the visa requirements for your nationality by visiting the Cook Islands Immigration Department's official website or contacting the closest Cook Islands embassy or consulate.

Immigration and Customs:

When you arrive in the Cook Islands, you must go through customs and immigration. Prepare your passport and other relevant travel papers for scrutiny.

Prepare to declare any restricted or forbidden products and follow customs laws.

Transportation to and from the hotel:

Rarotonga is a tiny island, and the majority of lodging choices are situated around the airport.

Many hotels and resorts provide airport transportation to their customers. If not, taxis and vehicle rentals are widely accessible, and automobile rentals may be scheduled at the airport or ahead of time.

Traveling Between Islands:

You may book domestic flights or organize ferry transfers from Rarotonga to other Cook Islands islands such as Aitutaki or Atiu.

Air Rarotonga, the national airline, operates domestic flights that provide easy connections to numerous islands. Certain routes may also be reached by ferry.

To get the greatest discounts and assure availability, book your flights well in advance, particularly during high travel seasons. Consider your travel dates' flexibility and compare costs from several airlines to discover the most convenient and cost-effective choices for your trip to the Cook Islands.

Average fares for flights to Cook Islands

Flights to the Cook Islands may vary in price based on criteria such as departure location, time of year, airline, and booking restrictions. It should be noted that these prices are subject to change and may vary depending on market circumstances. Here are some typical airfares to the Cook Islands from popular departure cities:

Flights departing from Auckland, New Zealand:

Air New Zealand provides nonstop service from Auckland to Rarotonga. Depending on the season and availability, round-trip flight prices might vary from roughly NZD 400 to NZD 800 or more.

It's worth noting that Air New Zealand sometimes provides special specials and promotions, so keeping a look out for such might help you get lower flights.

Flights departing from Sydney, Australia:

Round-trip airfare from Sydney to Rarotonga normally ranges from AUD 700 to AUD 1,200 or more. Prices might vary depending on the time of year, demand, and airline options.

Air New Zealand, Virgin Australia, and Qantas all operate connecting flights from Sydney to Rarotonga.

Flights from Los Angeles, California:

Round-trip flights from Los Angeles to Rarotonga often run from USD 900 to USD 1,500 or more. Prices might vary according on the airline, season, and early booking.

Air New Zealand offers direct flights from Los Angeles to Rarotonga, while Fiji Airways and Air Tahiti provide connecting flights with layovers at their respective hubs.

It's crucial to remember that these rates are only averages and might change depending on seasonality, demand, specials, and booking circumstances. It is advised that you check with multiple airlines and online travel firms that specialize in flights to the Cook Islands to acquire the most accurate and up-to-date costs. Furthermore, buying your tickets early and being flexible with your vacation dates will frequently help you locate better discounts and lower costs.

Getting to and from the Airport

When you arrive at Rarotonga International Airport in the Cook Islands, you have numerous alternatives for getting to your hotel or chosen location. The following are the primary modes of transportation:

Airport Transportation:

Many hotels and resorts in the Cook Islands provide airport transfers for its visitors. These transfers may be scheduled ahead of time or upon arrival.

At the airport's arrivals area, look for your hotel representative or certified transfer service workers. They will assist you in finding your transfer car.

Taxis:

At Rarotonga International Airport, taxis are easily accessible. The taxi rank is just outside the arrivals area.

The government regulates the rates, and there is a set tariff for transportation to various regions on the island. Before beginning the ride, confirm the fare with the driver.

Rental Cars:

Renting a vehicle is a popular way to explore the Cook Islands at your leisure. There are many automobile rental firms with counters at the airport.

It is best to reserve your automobile ahead of time to assure availability. Make sure you have a valid driver's license and are acquainted with the local driving laws.

Buses for the Public:

The Cook Islands provide a public bus service known as "The Island Bus" on Rarotonga. The bus station is just outside the airport.

The buses travel on a set schedule and service different destinations across the island. The bus fares are reasonable, and precise change is needed before boarding.

Private Transportation:

Private transfers may be pre-arranged via tour operators or transportation firms. These providers offer individual transportation to and from your lodging.

If you want a more personalized and private experience, private transports might be useful.

Consider considerations such as the location of your lodging, the number of persons going, your budget, and your preferences for ease and flexibility when choosing your mode of transportation. It's best to plan ahead of time, particularly during high travel seasons, to guarantee a seamless and trouble-free transfer from the airport to your selected location in the Cook Islands.

Moving Around the Islands

It is reasonably simple and convenient to get about the Cook Islands, especially on the major island of Rarotonga. The following are the major types of transportation for touring the islands:

Scooters and rental cars:

Renting a vehicle or scooter is a popular way to move about the Cook Islands, particularly on Rarotonga, the major island.

Several automobile rental firms provide a variety of vehicles for hire, including cars, scooters, and motorbikes, on a daily or weekly basis.

Having your own car allows you to explore the islands at your leisure and visit numerous attractions and picturesque areas.

Public transportation (The Island Bus):

Rarotonga offers a dependable public bus service known as "The Island Bus," which circles the island around and anticlockwise.

The buses follow a timetable and stop at popular spots such as beaches, resorts, shopping centers, and cultural attractions.

Bus rates are reasonable, however precise change is needed upon boarding. Timetables are available at the Visitor Information Centre or online.

Taxis:

Taxis may be found on the larger islands, particularly Rarotonga and Aitutaki.

Taxis may be flagged down on the street or booked via your hotel or a taxi company. Before beginning the ride, confirm the fare with the driver.

Walking and cycling:

Rarotonga is a tiny island that can easily navigated by foot or bicycle.

Cycling is a popular means of transportation on the island, and there are bike rental businesses where you may hire bicycles and enjoy the gorgeous coastline route.

Walking is also an alternative, especially for shorter distances and inside town.

Flights and ferries

Domestic flights or ferry services are available to neighboring Cook Islands islands such as Aitutaki and Atiu.

Domestic planes link the numerous islands, while ferries provide a picturesque and relaxing method of transportation on select routes.

Consider the distance you need to go, the number of people in your party, your budget, and your chosen degree of convenience and flexibility when organizing your transportation throughout the Cook Islands. It's a good idea to try out various kinds of transportation to get a taste of island life and make the most of your stay in the Cook Islands.

Modes of Public Transportation

The Cook Islands' public transportation system, notably on the major island of Rarotonga, is known as "The Island Bus." Here are some information concerning public transportation in the Cook Islands:

Rarotonga's Island Bus:

The Island Bus is Rarotonga's major means of public transportation, providing an inexpensive and easy way to go about the island.

The buses go around Rarotonga in both clockwise and anti-clockwise directions. They stop at authorized bus stations along the route on a regular basis.

The buses are comfy and air-conditioned, making for a pleasant journey.

Timetables and bus routes:

The Island Bus has a set schedule, with buses operating typically every hour in both directions.

The schedule is accessible online and in the Visitor Information Centre in Avarua, Rarotonga's capital.

The buses go in a circle around the island, stopping at popular spots like as resorts, beaches, shopping centers, and cultural institutions.

Payment and Fares:

The bus rates are reasonable, making it a cost-effective way to go about Rarotonga.

When boarding the bus, exact change is essential since drivers do not issue change.

Fares may vary depending on the distance traveled, with shorter trips costing less than longer trips.

Route adaptability:

The Island Bus enables you to get on and off at several points along the route, giving you the freedom to explore local sites and activities.

You may arrange your route around the bus schedule and spend as much time as you like at each stop before catching the next bus.

Local Advice:

It is best to be at the bus stop a few minutes before the official departure time to avoid missing the bus.

The Island Bus is popular among both residents and visitors, so plan your trip carefully during peak travel seasons or crowded periods to ensure a seat.

Using public transportation in the Cook Islands, such as The Island Bus, not only provides a cheap method to travel about, but also enables you to mingle with people and enjoy the laid-back attitude of the island. It's a terrific way to get about Rarotonga and see major attractions without having to hire a car.

Automobile Rentals

Car rentals are a popular and simple way to move about the Cook Islands, especially on Rarotonga, the major island. What you need to know about automobile rentals in the Cook Islands is as follows:

Rental Companies:

There are various automobile rental companies in the Cook Islands, both foreign and domestic.

International automobile rental firms like as Avis, Budget, and Europcar, as well as local rental providers, have a presence on the islands.

Rental Conditions:

You must be at least 21 years old and have a valid driver's license from your home country or an international driving permit (IDP) to hire a vehicle in the Cook Islands.

Some automobile rental companies may have age limitations or other criteria, so verify with the rental company ahead of time.

Advance Reservations:

It is important to reserve your rental vehicle ahead of time, particularly during high travel seasons, to assure availability and the best pricing.

You may book directly with the vehicle rental company or via online travel firms that specialize in car rentals.

Vehicle Alternatives:

Car rental companies in the Cook Islands provide a variety of vehicles to meet a variety of demands, including small cars, sedans, SUVs, and even vans.

When choosing a car, keep the size of your trip group and the quantity of baggage in mind.

How to Drive in the Cook Islands:

The Cook Islands follow New Zealand driving standards and drive on the left side of the road.

Before you drive, spend some time becoming acquainted with the local traffic laws and signs.

Rarotonga has a single major road that encircle the island, making navigating simple.

Insurance:

Car rental companies usually offer insurance for their cars. Inquire about the insurance alternatives available as well as any extra fees or excess costs.

Gas Stations:

There are various petrol stations on Rarotonga where you may fill up your rental vehicle.

Because there are fewer gasoline stations outside of the major cities, it's best to keep an eye on your fuel levels and plan your journeys appropriately.

Renting a vehicle in the Cook Islands allows you to go at your own speed and explore the islands at your leisure. It makes it easy to go to many sites, beaches, and vistas. However, it is essential to drive responsibly, follow local traffic restrictions, and preserve the natural environment while enjoying your Cook Islands car rental experience.

Scooters and Bicycles

Bicycles and scooters are prominent ways of mobility in the Cook Islands, particularly on Rarotonga, the major island. What you need to know about hiring bicycles and scooters is as follows:

Options for Rent:

Rarotonga has a number of rental outlets where you may hire bicycles and scooters.

These rental stores cater to both residents and visitors, and there are several alternatives to meet your interests and requirements.

Bicycles:

Renting a bicycle is an excellent way to explore Rarotonga at your own speed.

Bicycles come in a variety of forms, such as mountain bikes, cruiser bikes, and electric bikes.

Bicycle rental fees are often reasonable, and you may rent them for a few hours, a day, or even longer lengths of time.

Motorcycles and scooters:

Scooters and motorbikes are a quick and easy method to go about the island.

Rental businesses provide scooters and motorbikes with varying engine capacity to accommodate users of all skill levels and preferences.

To hire and ride a scooter or motorbike, you must have a valid driver's license.

Rental Conditions:

The rental regulations for bicycles and scooters may change across rental establishments.

You will often be required to present a valid identity document, such as a passport, as well as sign a rental agreement.

As security, certain rental businesses may request a deposit or a credit card authorisation.

Considerations for Safety:

Before hiring a bicycle or scooter, make sure you are comfortable riding and have a basic understanding of road safety.

Wear adequate safety equipment, like as helmets, to keep oneself safe when riding.

Learn the local traffic regulations and road conditions, and always ride defensively.

Rarotonga Exploration:

Rarotonga features a picturesque coastal road that encircles the island and provides spectacular views.

Bicycles and scooters enable you to go at your own leisure to beaches, cultural sites, and other attractions.

Rental Period and Fees:

Bicycle and scooter rental costs vary according on rental time and vehicle type.

Before making a reservation, it is best to enquire about rental pricing, including any extra fees or insurance choices.

In the Cook Islands, renting bicycles or scooters is a unique and entertaining way to explore the island's natural beauty and attractions. Whether you prefer the freedom of riding a bicycle or the ease of zipping about on a scooter, these alternatives enable you to immerse yourself in the laid-back attitude of the island and explore its hidden jewels at your own pace.

Trails for Walking and Hiking

Walking and hiking routes in the Cook Islands provide an excellent chance to explore the natural beauty of the islands, immerse yourself in the breathtaking scenery, and find hidden jewels. What you need to know about walking and hiking routes in the Cook Islands is as follows:

Walking Trails on Rarotonga:

Rarotonga, the major island, has a variety of walking trails to suit various fitness levels and interests.

One of the most popular routes, the Cross-Island Track, takes you from one side of the island to the other, going through thick rainforest, crossing streams, and providing stunning views.

Another picturesque path is the Raemaru Track, which leads to the peak of Raemaru Peak and provides panoramic views of the island.

Nature Trails in Aitutaki:

Aitutaki, noted for its beautiful lagoon, also features nature paths where you may learn about the island's distinctive flora and animals.

Walking through historic marae sites and beautiful scenery, the Punarei Cultural Track on Aitutaki provides insights into the island's history and traditional traditions.

The Atiu Eco-Trail:

Atiu, one of the Cook Islands' less-explored islands, has an Eco-Trail that winds through lush woods, limestone caverns, and agricultural regions.

The route highlights the island's ecology and provides opportunities to see local bird species such as the uncommon Kopeka (Atiu swiftlet).

Coastal Walk in Mangaia:

Mangaia, the southernmost inhabited island, has a beautiful coastline walk with views of steep cliffs, turquoise waves, and limestone caverns.

The stroll is an excellent chance to appreciate the island's natural beauty while also learning about its geological structures.

Considerations for Safety:

It is critical to emphasize safety while walking or hiking paths.

Wear adequate footwear, bring plenty of drink, and use sunscreen and a hat to protect yourself from the sun.

Inform someone of your intended path and approximate return time, particularly if you're hiking alone or on less-used routes.

Tour Guides and Local Knowledge:

Consider attending a guided tour if you want a more supervised experience or want to understand more about the flora, wildlife, and cultural importance of the paths.

With their understanding of the region, local guides may give vital insights and augment your hiking experience.

Accessibility and trail conditions:

Because trail conditions and accessibility might vary, it's best to get information about the route's present situation from visitor centers or local experts before heading out.

Some paths may need moderate fitness levels, so select those that match your ability and interests.

Walking and trekking in the Cook Islands enable you to interact with nature, enjoy the islands' distinctive landscapes, and experience their peacefulness and beauty up close and personal. Whether you're looking for a strenuous hike or a leisurely walk, the Cook Islands provide a variety of routes to fit your needs and offers amazing experiences for outdoor lovers.

Money and Currency Issues

When planning a vacation to the Cook Islands, it's essential to grasp the currency and money-related issues in order to have a pleasant financial experience. Here is some information on the Cook Islands' currency and money:

The Cook Islands' official currency is the New Zealand dollar (NZD). The Cook Islands use the same currency as New Zealand, with similar banknotes and coins.

Exchange Rate: The New Zealand dollar's exchange rate with other currencies might vary. Before your travel, check the current exchange rate to get an idea of the value of your native currency in respect to the NZD.

Cash and credit card payments are frequently accepted in the Cook Islands, particularly at local taverns, marketplaces, and small enterprises. Carry some cash with you for minor transactions and businesses that may not take credit or debit cards.

ATMs: Automated Teller Machines (ATMs) are present in the Cook Islands, mainly on Rarotonga, the biggest island, and Avarua, the capital. You may withdraw money using a debit or credit card. However, it is always a good idea to notify your bank of your trip intentions to ensure that you have continuous access to your cash.

Credit and Debit Cards: Most hotels, resorts, restaurants, and bigger enterprises take major credit and debit cards such as Visa and Mastercard. However, carrying some cash as a backup is still advisable, particularly when visiting smaller businesses, markets, or rural places where card capabilities may be restricted.

Money Exchange: Foreign money may be exchanged for New Zealand dollars at banks and currency exchange bureaus. However, bear in mind that currency exchange facilities on the smaller islands may be restricted, so it's best to convert money before coming to the Cook Islands or upon arrival at the international airport.

Traveler's checks: Traveler's checks are not generally recognized in the Cook Islands, and finding somewhere to cash them may be difficult. It is advisable to use cash or credit cards for your transactions.

Tipping is not often practiced in the Cook Islands. A little tip may be provided if you get great service or wish to express thanks, but it is not required.

Taxes: A products and Services Tax (GST) is levied on the pricing of products and services in the Cook Islands. The current interest rate is 15%. pricing are normally given with GST included, so there are no extra taxes on top of the mentioned pricing.

Budgeting: The cost of living in the Cook Islands might be greater than in other places. It is best to plan and budget ahead of time, taking into account accommodation, food, transportation, activities, and any other costs you may incur during your visit.

Keep your money and valuables safe during your vacation. Use hotel safes or other secure storage solutions for big sums of cash, and be careful while transporting significant amounts of cash. You may secure a hassle-free financial experience and enjoy your stay in this lovely place by being prepared and knowing the currency and money problems in the Cook Islands.

Visa Requirements

The Cook Islands visa requirements vary based on your nationality, as well as the purpose and length of your travel. Here are some key aspects to consider:

Visa-Free Entry: Citizens of several nations, including the United States, Canada, the United Kingdom, Australia, and the majority of European Union countries, are not required to get a visa to visit the

Cook Islands for tourist reasons. When they arrive, they are given a visitor permit that permits them to remain for up to 31 days.

Extension of remain: If you want to remain longer than the original 31-day term, you may apply to the Cook Islands Immigration Department for an extension of stay. Extensions are normally given for up to 31 days, allowing for a total stay of up to 62 days.

Work Permits: If you want to work in the Cook Islands, you must first get a work permit. Work permits are only granted for specified employment positions and must be sponsored by a Cook Islands company. The application procedure requires the submission of supporting papers such as evidence of credentials, a job offer, and health tests.

Student Visas: If you want to study in the Cook Islands, you must first get a student visa. Acceptance into a recognized educational institution in the Cook Islands is required, as are particular visa requirements. For further information on application processes, contact the institution or the Cook Islands Immigration Department.

Business Visas: If you are visiting the Cook Islands for business activities, such as attending conferences, meetings, or looking into prospective investment possibilities, you may be required to apply for a business visa. A letter of invitation or other supporting documentation from a host organization in the Cook Islands are normally required for business visas.

Regardless of visa restrictions, all travelers to the Cook Islands must have a valid passport valid for at least six months beyond the anticipated departure date. Before going, make sure your passport is still valid.

Travelers in Transit: If you are passing through the Cook Islands on your way to another location, you may be free from visa requirements if you have onward travel tickets and do not remain for more than 24 hours. It is, nevertheless, suggested that you verify with your airline and the Cook Islands Immigration Department to confirm that you are in compliance with transit rules.

It's important to note that visa requirements and regulations can change, so check the Cook Islands Immigration Department's official website or contact the nearest Cook Islands embassy or consulate in your country for the most up-to-date information on visa requirements for your nationality.

Processes of Acquiring a visa to the Cook Islands

Determine the sort of Visa: Determine the sort of visa you need depending on your visit's purpose, such as a tourist, work, student, or business visa. Each visa class has its own set of criteria and accompanying documentation.

Gather Required papers: Gather all required papers in accordance with the criteria of your selected visa type. A completed visa application form, a valid passport with sufficient validity, recent passport-sized photographs, proof of travel arrangements (e.g., return ticket), proof of accommodation, proof of financial means to support your stay, and any other documents specific to your visa category (e.g., job offer letter for work visa) are typically required.

Complete the Visa Application Form: Obtain the visa application form from the official website of the Cook Islands

Immigration Department or from the Cook Islands embassy or consulate in your country. Fill out the form completely and ensure that all mandatory fields are filled out.

Pay Visa Application costs: Determine the visa application costs that apply to your visa type and pay them. Payment methods may differ, therefore see the Cook Islands Immigration Department or the embassy/consulate for details.

Submit Your Application: To the specified office, submit your completed visa application form together with the necessary supporting papers. Depending on the exact processes in place, this may include filing your application in person at the Cook Islands Immigration Department, the local Cook Islands embassy or consulate, or through an online application site.

Wait for Processing: After completing your application, you must wait for the visa to be processed. Because processing durations vary, it is best to apply well in advance of your anticipated trip dates. The immigration authorities will assess your application and accompanying documentation during this period.

Attend Interviews or supply Biometrics (if needed): As part of the application process, you may be needed to attend an interview or supply biometric data (such as fingerprints or pictures) depending on the kind of visa and your circumstances. Follow any further necessary instructions supplied by the Cook Islands Immigration Department or embassy/consulate.

You will be informed of the decision on your visa application after it has been processed. If your application is granted, you will get your visa in the form of a passport sticker or an electronic visa (e-visa). If your application is rejected, you will be notified of the reasons why.

Plan Your Trip: Once you have received your visa, make plans to visit the Cook Islands. Make plans for flights, lodging, and other parts of your vacation.

It's vital to note that the preceding stages are just a general guideline; individual needs and processes may differ. For the most current and up-to-date information on the visa application procedure, always consult official sources such as the Cook Islands Immigration Department or the local Cook Islands embassy or consulate.

CHAPTER 3: Accommodation Options in Cook Islands

Hotels and Resorts

The Cook Islands' resorts and hotels provide a wide range of lodging alternatives to suit a variety of budgets, interests, and travel types. Here's everything you need to know about Cook Islands resorts and hotels:

Resort Excursions

The Cook Islands include a variety of resorts that offer tourists a rich and indulgent experience.

Private beaches, swimming pools, spa facilities, on-site restaurants, bars, and recreational activities are common attractions in resorts.

These accommodations are suitable for guests looking for a pleasant and soothing stay with easy access to amenities and services.4

Hotel Choices:

Hotels in the Cook Islands range in size and design, from boutique to bigger, well-established resorts.

Hotels usually provide pleasant accommodations, on-site restaurants, and facilities like swimming pools and exercise centers.

Depending on the hotel, extra amenities such as beach access, water sports facilities, or cultural events may be available.

Considerations for Location:

The Cook Islands have a variety of lodging alternatives on several islands.

Rarotonga, the major island, has a diverse range of resorts and hotels, including those on the coast and in lush, tropical surroundings.

Aitutaki, famous for its stunning lagoon, also has magnificent resorts with direct access to its crystal-clear seas.

Budget-Friendly Alternatives:

If you're on a limited budget, there are even more cheap hotels, guesthouses, and backpacker lodgings.

These alternatives provide simple facilities and decent housing, making them ideal for individuals who want to spend more time touring the islands and less time in their accommodations.

Accommodations for Self-Catering:

Self-catering accommodations, such as vacation houses, villas, and flats, are another option to explore.

These choices allow you to prepare your own meals and are suitable for longer stays or visitors looking for a more autonomous experience.

Considerations for Booking:

It is important to book your accommodations ahead of time, particularly during busy travel seasons, to assure availability and the best pricing.

Various online travel firms and hotel booking systems provide a diverse choice of possibilities.

Furthermore, contacting the resort or hotel directly may result in greater rates or customised packages.

Stays for Cultural Purposes:

Consider staying in a family-run guesthouse or participating in a cultural homestay program for a really immersed experience.

These alternatives allow you to engage with people, learn about Cook Islands customs and lifestyle, and obtain a better grasp of the local culture.

Consider your budget, chosen location, desired facilities, and the kind of experience you want when choosing a resort or hotel in the Cook Islands. With so many possibilities, you're sure to discover the right lodging that meets your preferences and enriches your entire experience in the beautiful Cook Islands.

Best Places to Stay in the Cook Islands

The Cook Islands include a few different regions where you may stay, each with its own distinct qualities and attraction. The following are some of the top places to stay in the Cook Islands:

Muri Beach, Rarotonga:

- Muri Beach is a popular destination for tourists to Rarotonga, the Cook Islands' major island.

- This region has a beautiful lagoon with crystal-clear waters that is great for swimming, snorkeling, and other water activities.
- Muri Beach has a variety of lodging choices, including resorts, hotels, and self-catering alternatives.
- The neighborhood also has a number of restaurants, cafés, and stores, making it a handy and lively location to stay.

Avarua - Rarotonga:

- Avarua, the Cook Islands' capital, is situated on Rarotonga's northern shore.
- Staying at Avarua puts you close to the island's administrative and economic centers, as well as cultural sites such as the Cook Islands National Museum.
- The neighborhood has a variety of lodging alternatives, ranging from low-cost options to boutique hotels.
- Avarua is particularly well-known for the lively Punanga Nui Market, which sells local fruit, crafts, and souvenirs.

Aitutaki Lagoon - Aitutaki:

- Aitutaki, known for its stunning lagoon, is a favorite location for people looking for a peaceful and scenic getaway.

- Staying near Aitutaki Lagoon enables you to take in the breathtaking scenery, relax on beautiful beaches, and participate in water sports like as snorkeling and kayaking.
- The region has a number of upscale resorts and hotels with direct access to the lagoon.

Teenui Village - Atiu:

- Atiu is a less-visited Cook Islands island that provides a more off-the-beaten-path experience.
- Teenui Village, noted for its gorgeous surroundings and accessibility to natural attractions, is a perfect place to stay on Atiu.
- The region has guesthouses and hotels that allow you to immerse yourself in the local culture while also exploring the island's distinctive surroundings.

Private Islands and Resorts on Other Islands:

- Aside from Rarotonga and Aitutaki, the Cook Islands contain a number of smaller islands that provide private and intimate experiences.
- Private islands and resorts, such as those on One Foot Island and the opulent homes on Motu Tapu, provide a more intimate and luxurious vacation in the midst of pure natural beauty.

- Consider your choices for beach access, facilities, closeness to attractions, and the sort of experience you wish to have when picking where to stay in the Cook Islands. Each place has its own personality, and no matter where you stay, you'll be able to experience the Cook Islands' natural beauty and kind welcome.

Areas to Avoid in Cook Islands

The Cook Islands are typically safe and hospitable to tourists, but like with any location, there may be places or circumstances where visitors should take care. Here are a few things to keep in mind when visiting the Cook Islands:

Areas that are remote or uninhabited:

The Cook Islands have several deserted or isolated locations, particularly on the outlying islands.

Because these locations may lack infrastructure, amenities, and emergency aid, it's best to be cautious and avoid travelling into distant areas without sufficient preparation or advice.

Trails that are unmarked or unofficial:

It's important to adhere to recognized pathways and approved trails while visiting hiking trails and natural regions.

Unmarked regions should be avoided because they may have dangerous terrain, concealed dangers, or private property.

Evening Activities:

When partaking in evening activities, like with other place, practice prudence.

Stay in well-lit, crowded locations and be aware of your surroundings.

Avoid going alone at night in unfamiliar or poorly lighted locations.

Unattended Beach Valuables:

While the Cook Islands are typically secure, it's always a good idea to keep an eye on your valuables, particularly on beaches.

When swimming or sunbathing, never leave your belongings unattended.

When required, use lockers or hotel safes to safeguard your possessions.

Excessive drinking may impair judgment and personal safety.

It's best to drink sensibly and stay under your limitations, particularly while participating in aquatic sports or touring new places.

Highway Safety:

Follow local traffic rules and regulations whether driving or using public transit.

Be mindful of road conditions, especially if it is raining or storming.

Avoid driving when impaired by drink or drugs.

Cultural Awareness:

The Cook Islands feature a vibrant Polynesian culture, and it is important to respect local customs and traditions.

When visiting communities or religious locations, dress modestly and get permission before photographing persons or cultural events.

While visiting the Cook Islands, it is essential to apply common sense, be aware of your surroundings, and take the required measures. While the majority of the islands are safe, it's always a good idea to be cautious and follow local advice to guarantee a nice and safe vacation.

Inns and Bed and Breakfasts

Guesthouses and bed and breakfasts in the Cook Islands provide a more intimate and customized experience for visitors. Here's everything you need to know about Cook Islands guesthouses and bed and breakfasts:

Genuine Local Experience:

Guesthouses and bed and breakfasts allow you to immerse yourself in the local culture and way of life.

These establishments are often owned by local families or individuals who provide warm hospitality and insight into Cook Islands traditions and customs.

Staying at a guesthouse or bed and breakfast enables you to interact with the locals and obtain a better knowledge of the area.

Atmosphere that is both comfortable and cozy:

Guesthouses and bed and breakfasts often provide nice and comfortable lodging.

Individually designed rooms with a homey atmosphere provide a warm and welcome ambience for visitors.

Many guesthouses and bed and breakfasts feature communal spaces where visitors may relax and engage with other tourists or the owners, such as lounges or gardens.

Meals Prepared at Home:

The ability to taste cooked, traditional meals is one of the delights of visiting in a guesthouse or bed and breakfast.

Many hosts provide breakfast as part of the hotel package, which makes for a delightful start to the day.

Some guesthouses may also provide supplementary meals, enabling you to enjoy fresh-prepared local specialties.

Personalized Service and Recommendations from Locals:

Guesthouse and bed and breakfast owners are often knowledgeable about the region and may provide insider insights and suggestions.

They can advise you on the greatest local sights, hidden jewels, and off-the-beaten-path activities.

The customized attention and readiness to assist provided by the hosts may improve your entire stay and help you make the most of your time in the Cook Islands.

Budget-Friendly Alternative:

Guesthouses and bed and breakfasts in the Cook Islands are often inexpensive lodging alternatives for budget-conscious guests.

In comparison to bigger resorts or hotels, these enterprises provide a more pleasant and genuine experience at a lower cost.

Staying at a guesthouse or bed and breakfast helps you to save money on lodging, which you can use towards other areas of your trip, such as visiting the islands or participating in activities.

Consider variables such as location, facilities, reviews, and the special experiences or services given by the host when choosing a Cook Islands guesthouse or bed and breakfast. Each guesthouse or bed and breakfast has its own distinct personality, and staying in one of these establishments may give an enriching and memorable visit that embodies the warmth and friendliness of the Cook Islands.

Self-Catering Facilities

Self-catering lodgings in the Cook Islands provide tourists who like their own space and the opportunity to make their own meals a flexible and autonomous choice. Here's what you should know about self-catering lodging in the Cook Islands:

Various Options:

Holiday houses, villas, flats, and bungalows are examples of self-catering lodgings in the Cook Islands.

These accommodations are available in a variety of sizes and types to accommodate a wide range of party sizes and budgets.

There are beachfront villas, isolated retreats, and lodgings situated in beautiful tropical surroundings to select from.

Facilities that are fully equipped:

The utilities required for a pleasant stay are provided in self-catering lodgings.

A kitchen or kitchenette with cooking supplies and appliances, as well as eating rooms, are common features of facilities.

Having a kitchen enables you to cook your own meals and snacks, which is more convenient and perhaps cheaper than eating out every time.

Privacy and flexibility:

Self-catering rooms provide a high degree of solitude as well as the flexibility to organize your own schedule.

You can relax in your own space, with separate living rooms and private outside spaces like balconies or gardens.

This sort of lodging is great for families, parties, or individuals that appreciate privacy and the opportunity to relax in a home-like setting.

Exploration of the Local Market:

Staying in a self-catering property allows you to visit local markets and food shops.

You may buy fresh vegetables, local ingredients, and specialities to make your own meals and sample the local cuisine.

As you mingle with the local population and enjoy local cuisines, this adds a cultural and interactive aspect to your stay.

Option with the Best Value:

Self-catering lodgings may be an economical option, particularly for longer stays or bigger parties.

You may save money on dining expenditures and get more control over your food budget by making your own meals.

Furthermore, self-catering accommodations are sometimes less expensive than standard hotels or resorts.

Local Assistance and Services:

In the Cook Islands, self-catering lodgings are often maintained by local property owners or managers.

They may provide guidance, suggestions, and local knowledge to ensure a pleasant and pleasurable visit.

Some lodgings may include extra services such as cleaning, laundry facilities, and activity and tour planning.

When looking for self-catering accommodation in the Cook Islands, examine the location, facilities, reviews, and booking information. It's also a good idea to connect directly with the property owner or management to clear up any confusion and check that the accommodation suits your unique requirements. Self-catering lodgings provide the conveniences of a home away from home while giving a convenient and autonomous way to see the Cook Islands.

Budget friendly, Mid-ranged, and Luxury Hostels on Cook Island.

The Cook Islands provide a variety of hostels to suit a variety of budgets and interests. There are alternatives available whether you are a budget traveler searching for economical lodgings or a more premium hostel experience. Here is a list of cheap, mid-range, and luxury hostels in the Cook Islands, along with their typical costs and locations:

Hostels on a Budget:

a) International Backpackers Hostel:

Avarua, Rarotonga is the location.

The average nightly rate is $20-30.

Description: This hostel is located in the centre of Avarua, the Cook Islands' capital. It provides dorm-style rooms with common bathrooms. The hostel has a shared kitchen, a sitting room, and outdoor seating. It's a low-cost choice for guests searching for modest rooms in a convenient location.

The Backpackers of Rarotongan:

Arorangi, Rarotonga is the location.

The average nightly rate is $25-35.

This hostel, located near the picturesque Arorangi Beach, provides dormitory accommodations as well as individual rooms with communal toilets. The hostel has a shared kitchen, social spaces, and a large outside patio. It's a popular alternative for travellers looking for cheap lodging near the beach.

Hostels in the Middle Class:

a) Hotel Muri Beach Club:

Muri Beach, Rarotonga is the location.

The average nightly rate is $150-200.

This budget hostel is situated on the beautiful Muri Beach. It has individual rooms with ensuite bathrooms that are nice. The hostel has a swimming pool, direct beach access, a restaurant, and a bar.

It's an excellent alternative for tourists looking for a good mix of cost and comfort.

Private Island Resort Aitutaki Lagoon:

Akitua Island is located in Aitutaki.

The average nightly rate is $300-400.

This mid-range hostel is located on a private island in the beautiful Aitutaki Lagoon and provides attractive bungalows and beachside lodgings. The hostel has a restaurant, a bar, a spa, and a variety of aquatic sports. It's a popular option for visitors looking for a relaxed and scenic vacation in a peaceful area.

Luxurious Hostels:

Rarotonga Pacific Resort:

Muri Beach, Rarotonga is the location.

The average nightly rate is $400-500.

This luxurious hostel is situated on the picturesque Muri Beach. It has rooms that are big and attractively built, with contemporary conveniences and private balconies. The hostel has a swimming pool, spa, several food choices, and direct beach access. It's a great option for those looking for a lavish and sumptuous vacation.

The Rarotongan Luxury Resort & Spa:

This resort is located on the island of Rarotongan.

Aroa Beach, Rarotonga is the location.

The average nightly rate is $500-600.

This premium hostel, located on the picturesque Aroa Beach, provides expensive rooms and suites with spectacular ocean views. The hostel has a spa, many restaurants, swimming pools, water sports, and a kids' club. It's an excellent choice for anyone looking for a luxurious and unforgettable stay on the beach.

Please keep in mind that the rates shown are averages and may vary based on the season, availability, and room type. For the most current and up-to-date price information, check with each hostel directly or via online booking platforms.

Backpacking and camping

Camping and backpacking in the Cook Islands provide adventurous tourists with a one-of-a-kind opportunity to discover the islands' natural beauty and immerse themselves in the breathtaking sceneries. What you need to know about camping and backpacking in the Cook Islands is as follows:

Permits for Camping:

It is necessary to get a camping permission from the Cook Islands Ministry of Cultural Development or the applicable municipal authorities before setting up camp.

Camping permits guarantee that you are adhering to the government's rules and norms, as well as helping to preserve the natural environment.

Campgrounds and other amenities:

Camping is allowed in selected campsites in the Cook Islands. Toilets, showers, and grilling spaces are available at these campsites.

Some campsites may include extra amenities such as picnic tables, grills, and access to water supplies.

It's a good idea to research each campground's individual amenities and prepare appropriately.

Supplies and equipment:

You must carry your own camping equipment if you want to camp or backpack in the Cook Islands.

A tent, sleeping bag, sleeping pad, cooking utensils, and food supplies are all required.

Pack lightweight and compact camping supplies appropriate for tropical regions.

Never Leave a Trace:

When camping or hiking in the Cook Islands, it is essential to adhere to the Leave No Trace guidelines.

This includes leaving campsites in the same condition you found them, appropriately disposing of rubbish, and preserving the natural environment.

Be cautious of the fragile ecosystems and cultural places, and avoid causing harm or disturbance to them.

Considerations for Safety:

When camping or trekking in the Cook Islands, put safety first.

Keep an eye out for weather conditions, such as tropical storms or cyclones, and take the required preparations.

Keep emergency contact information and a first-aid kit on hand.

It's also a good idea to let someone know about your intentions, including your preferred camping area and projected length of stay.

Respect local customs and communities:

Respect the traditions and privacy of surrounding towns and villages while camping nearby.

If you're camping on private property, be sure you get permission from the landowners.

Dress modestly and keep local cultural norms and sensitivities in mind.

Alternative Accommodation Possibilities:

If camping isn't your thing, you may still backpack in the Cook Islands by staying in affordable lodgings like guesthouses or hostels.

These alternatives provide a pleasant and cheap location to stay while exploring the islands.

While camping and backpacking provide a feeling of independence and adventure, they may not be ideal for everyone. It requires self-sufficiency, outdoor abilities, and a daring mentality. Always plan your camping or backpacking trip ahead of time, taking into account local rules, weather conditions, and safety procedures.

Travel Protection

Travel insurance is an important part of every journey, including trips to the Cook Islands. It gives financial security and peace of mind in the event of unforeseen disasters or crises. Here's everything you need to know about Cook Islands travel insurance:

Medical Emergencies Coverage:

Medical expenditures, such as hospitalization, doctor's appointments, and drugs, are often covered by travel insurance.

Because healthcare expenditures might be expensive in the Cook Islands, it's essential that your insurance policy covers medical emergencies.

Repatriation and evacuation:

Travel insurance may cover the expenses of a major sickness or accident that necessitates medical evacuation to another nation or repatriation back to your own country.

This coverage is critical, particularly in distant places with few sophisticated medical facilities.

Cancellation or interruption of a trip:

Travel insurance may financially cover you if your vacation is canceled or interrupted due to unexpected events such as sickness, natural catastrophes, or airline difficulties.

It may cover non-refundable charges such as plane tickets, hotel reservations, and pre-paid activities.

Baggage Lost or Delayed:

Travel insurance may cover lost, stolen, or damaged luggage while on vacation.

It may also cover the cost of required purchases if your luggage is delayed for a lengthy period of time.

Individual Liability:

Personal liability coverage, which covers you if you accidently cause property damage or harm someone while traveling, may be included in your travel insurance.

Coverage of Adventure Activities and Sports:

If you want to participate in adventurous activities or sports in the Cook Islands, be sure your travel insurance covers them.

Due to the hazards involved, certain hobbies, such as scuba diving, snorkeling, or trekking, may need supplementary coverage.

Read the Policy and Know Your Coverage:

Before getting travel insurance, read the policy paperwork thoroughly to ensure that you understand the coverage, exclusions, and claim processes.

Pay attention to any pre-existing medical problems that may influence coverage and, if required, consider acquiring supplemental coverage.

It is essential that you evaluate several travel insurance policies to pick the one that best meets your requirements.

Consider coverage limitations, deductibles, exclusions, and customer feedback.

Check to see whether the insurance company provides a dependable 24/7 emergency support hotline that you may call in an emergency.

Remember to get travel insurance prior to your trip to the Cook Islands to guarantee that you are covered from the minute you leave. While travel insurance increases the expense of your trip, it offers important safety and assistance in the event of an emergency, enabling you to enjoy your holiday with peace of mind.

User

Packing Suggestions

Pack sensibly when planning a vacation to the Cook Islands to ensure you have all you need for a comfortable and pleasurable stay. Consider the following packing suggestions:

Clothing that is light and breathable:

Because the Cook Islands have a warm, tropical environment, bring lightweight, breathable clothes like cotton or linen.

Items such as shorts, t-shirts, sundresses, swimsuits, and lightweight slacks or skirts should be included.

For sun protection, bring a hat, sunglasses, and a lightweight, long-sleeved shirt.

Swimwear and Beach Accessories:

Pack many swimsuits since you will most likely spend a lot of time enjoying the wonderful beaches and aquatic activities.

Bring a beach towel, flip-flops or sandals, and a beach bag to store your beach needs.

Protection against the sun:

In the Cook Islands, sunscreen is a necessary. Pack a sunscreen with a high SPF to protect your skin from the harsh tropical sun.

Bring a broad-brimmed hat, sunglasses, and a rash guard or lightweight cover-up for additional sun protection.

Repellent for insects:

Although the Cook Islands do not have a lot of mosquitos or insects, it's still a good idea to bring bug repellent with you for extra protection, particularly if you intend on exploring nature trails or in the nighttime.

Water Sports and Snorkeling:

If you want to snorkel or participate in aquatic sports, consider bringing your own snorkeling equipment, such as a mask, snorkel, and fins, for a more pleasant and sanitary experience.

If you want to travel light, most snorkeling equipment may be rented on the islands from diving shops or tour operators.

Outdoor Equipment and Accessories:

If you want to enjoy the natural splendor of the Cook Islands, bring appropriate walking shoes or hiking boots, depending on your plans.

During your outdoor travels, bring a day bag to hold basics such as water, food, a camera, and other personal stuff.

Adapters and Chargers for Travel:

Because the Cook Islands utilize Type I electrical outlets, bring a travel adaptor for your electronic equipment.

Remember to bring chargers for your phone, camera, and other electrical devices.

First Aid and Medications:

If you need prescription drugs, make sure you bring enough for the length of your vacation.

Consider carrying a basic first aid kit with necessities like bandages, antibacterial ointment, pain killers, and any drugs you may need.

Copies of travel documents:

Pack your passport, travel insurance paperwork, airline tickets, and any other required travel documents.

It's also a good idea to retain digital duplicates of these papers in case they become misplaced or stolen.

Cards and cash:

While credit cards are commonly accepted at most places in the Cook Islands, it's best to have extra cash on hand for smaller shops or regions where card acceptance is restricted.

Inform your bank of your trip intentions to prevent card complications while overseas.

Items of Interest:

A reusable water bottle, a travel umbrella, a travel guidebook or maps, a camera or waterproof phone cover, and any personal toiletries or prescriptions are also recommended.

Remember to pack light and keep your airline's weight limits in mind. Because the environment in the Cook Islands is easygoing and informal, consider comfort and adaptability in your outfit selections. You'll be well-prepared to make the most of your vacation to the Cook Islands with careful preparation and packing.

Beaches and Water Sports:

- **Snorkeling and Diving:** The Cook Islands have spectacular coral reefs and crystal-clear seas, making it an ideal snorkeling and diving destination.
- Discover vibrant marine life, coral gardens, and underwater caverns at popular snorkeling and diving destinations like as Aitutaki and Rarotonga. Dive companies provide guided trips as well as certification training for both novice and experienced divers.

Swimming and Sunbathing:

The Cook Islands have magnificent beaches with silky white sands and turquoise seas that are perfect for swimming and sunbathing.

-Relax on world-famous beaches such as Muri Beach, Titikaveka Beach, and One Foot Island. In a calm beach environment, enjoy the warm Pacific seas and soak up the sun.

Sailing and Kayaking:

Rent a kayak or join a sailing expedition to explore the lagoons and stunning coasts of the Cook Islands.

- Glide across the tranquil seas, find hidden beaches, and take in the breathtaking natural splendor. Sailing and kayaking provide a distinct viewpoint and enable you to visit secluded locations.

Cultural Encounters:

Visiting Traditional communities: - Immerse yourself in the rich Polynesian culture of the Cook Islands by visiting traditional communities.

Interact with the people, learn about their culture, and see traditional crafts, music, and dance performances.

- Enjoy the kind warmth and genuine spirit of the local villages.

Attending Traditional rituals:

- Participate in traditional rituals such as church services, cultural festivals, or traditional dance performances.

- Behold the vivid costumes, rhythmic dances, and beautiful music that highlight the Cook Islands' unique heritage.7

Outdoor Activities:

Hiking and Trekking: Embark on hiking and trekking trips to explore the lush landscapes and picturesque pathways of the Cook Islands.

Hike the Te Rua Manga (The Needle) trail in Rarotonga or explore the interior of Aitutaki for stunning views. - Along the route, discover secret waterfalls, difficult terrain, and panoramic panoramas.

Mountain bike and Cycling: - Rent a bicycle or join a mountain bike tour to explore the islands at your leisure.

- For a thrilling experience, cycle along coastal roads, past quaint towns, or face rugged off-road routes.

Fishing and Deep-Sea Angling: The Cook Islands provide fantastic fishing possibilities, including deep-sea angling.

Try your luck at catching marlin, tuna, mahi-mahi, and other game species by joining a fishing charter.

Enjoy the excitement of the pursuit as well as the gratifying sensation of landing a large fish.

Natural and Historical Landmarks:

Cook Islands National Museum: Learn about the islands' history, culture, and natural heritage at the Cook Islands National Museum in Rarotonga.

Explore relics, traditional crafts, and displays that highlight the island's Polynesian heritage.

Arai Te Tonga (Ancient Marae): - Visit Arai Te Tonga, an ancient marae (holy spot) on Atiu.

Discover the importance of this cultural monument and its traditional religious activities.

Te Rua Manga (The Needle): - Hike to Te Rua Manga, a remarkable rock feature resembling a needle in Rarotonga's center. From the peak, enjoy panoramic views of the island and take unique images.

Markets and Shopping:

Explore local markets and stores for one-of-a-kind souvenirs, handicrafts, and regional items.

Visit Rarotonga's Punanga Nui Market for fresh vegetables, arts and crafts, clothes, and local specialties.

Dining and Culinary Arts:

Enjoy the tastes of Cook Islands cuisine, which blends Polynesian and foreign influences.

Try ika mata (raw fish marinated in lime juice and coconut cream) and rukau (boiled taro leaves), two traditional meals.

Discover a variety of eating alternatives, ranging from informal coastal cafés to sophisticated dining places.

Entertainment and Nightlife:

Enjoy the Cook Islands' bustling nightlife scene, notably on Rarotonga.

Live music performances, cultural events, and dance parties are all available.

Interact with locals and other visitors while enjoying the vibrant atmosphere of the island's pubs and nightclubs.

Visitors to the Cook Islands may enjoy a wide selection of activities and experiences. The Cook Islands provide something for everyone, whether you're looking for leisure on the lovely beaches, adventure in the vast outdoors, or cultural immersion.

Music and Dance

Dance and music are important components of the Cook Islands' cultural fabric. The islands' bright and expressive traditional dance styles are complemented by rhythmic drumming and beautiful singing. Here is an overview of Cook Islands dance and music:

Dance Traditions:

- The Cook Islands are well-known for their traditional dance, the 'ura. It is a compelling and dynamic dancing style that both men and women may execute.
- The 'ura uses fluid motions, beautiful hand gestures, and sophisticated footwork to tell tales about love, nature, and everyday life.
- Dancers use brightly colored costumes embellished with traditional motifs and natural materials, producing a visually beautiful show.

Instruments and music:

- Music is an important aspect of Cook Islands culture, often accompanying traditional dances and festivities.

- The pate, a traditional drum built from a hollowed-out tree stump coated with sharkskin, is the principal instrument used in Cook Islands music.
- The ukulele, guitar, and pahu (a huge drum) are other traditional instruments. These instruments are used to compose melodic songs that are used to accompany dance performances.

Chants and Drumming:

- Drumming is an important part of Cook Islands music and dancing. The drummers' thunderous rhythms establish the rhythm and propel the dancers' motions.
- Chants, known as 'imene tuki,' are often used in performances. These chants, which are accompanied by rhythmic clapping, serve as a melodious background to the dancing routines.

Cultural Importance:

- Dance and music are very important culturally in the Cook Islands. They are viewed as a method to preserve and commemorate the islands' unique history and customs.
- Traditional dance performances serve as a vehicle for passing down cultural information and values from one generation to the next.

- Visitors to the Cook Islands may see these enthralling acts during cultural events, festivals, and scheduled shows.

Learning and Participation:

- There are courses and lessons available for individuals interested in experiencing Cook Islands dance and music firsthand.
- Dance courses provide an opportunity to master fundamental movements, comprehend the cultural importance of the dances, and dress in traditional clothing.
- These engaging programs provide tourists a better understanding of Cook Islands culture and enable them to interact with the local population.

Attending Cultural Exhibitions:

- Cultural events and shows are a big draw for tourists visiting the Cook Islands. These performances often include traditional dance, music, and storytelling.
- Various locations and resorts provide cultural nights where visitors may enjoy live performances, traditional food, and learn about the local culture.
- Dance and music are important to the Cook Islands' identity and give a window into the islands' rich cultural past. The bright dances and rhythmic music are a must-see for

anybody looking for an intensive cultural experience in the Cook Islands.

Art & Crafts

Art and crafts have a significant position in the Cook Islands' cultural history. The islands are famous for their one-of-a-kind and complex workmanship, with an emphasis on traditional Polynesian patterns and materials. Here is an overview of the Cook Islands' art and craft scene:

Traditional Arts and Crafts:

- Traditional crafts in the Cook Islands are strongly ingrained in the islanders' cultural heritage and have been handed down through centuries.
- Tivaevae: Tivaevae is a traditional type of quilting in which elaborate patterns are hand-stitched onto cloth. These exquisitely created quilts often include flowers, vegetation, and meaningful designs.
- Weaving is a popular craft in the Cook Islands, with materials such as pandanus leaves, coconut fronds, and kikau (dry coconut palm leaf) employed. Baskets, hats,

mats, and fans are among the traditional goods that are expertly weaved.

- Carving: Another traditional Cook Islands art is wood carving. Carving intricate motifs into wood creates beautiful sculptures, masks, and ceremonial artifacts.

Art of the Present:

- The Cook Islands also has a vibrant modern art culture, with local artists working in a variety of media and genres.
- Paintings: Many local painters use their paintings to capture the spectacular landscapes, seascapes, and cultural elements of the Cook Islands. The beauty and soul of the islands are captured in these works of art.
- Sculptures: Talented artists construct sculptures from wood, stone, or other materials, frequently with Polynesian themes and symbolism.
- Jewelry: The Cook Islands' jewelry is highly appreciated, with traditional styles and materials such of black pearls, shells, and native jewels. These one-of-a-kind sculptures are memorable and wearable mementos.

Cultural Importance:

- Art and crafts are inextricably linked to the Cook Islands' cultural character. They are used to preserve and convey cultural traditions, legends, and beliefs.
- Traditional patterns and symbols, such as the frangipani flower, fish hooks, and tiki figures, are often included into artwork and crafts to signify cultural value and ancestors.

Art & craft shopping:

- There are several possibilities for visitors visiting the Cook Islands to discover and buy native art and crafts.
- Local markets, such as Rarotonga's Punanga Nui Market, provide a broad variety of handicrafts, artwork, and traditional goods manufactured by local craftsmen.
- Galleries and shops: Throughout the islands, several art galleries and shops highlight the works of local artists, offering a selected variety of paintings, sculptures, and jewelry.

Helping Local Artists:

- Visitors may directly support the incomes of Cook Islands artists and help to the preservation of traditional craftsmanship by buying art and crafts from local craftsmen.

- Interacting with artists, visiting workshops, or taking part in cultural activities may provide insights into the creative processes and stories behind the artwork.

The Cook Islands' art and crafts provide a look into the inhabitants' rich cultural history and creative traditions. Exploring and admiring the local art scene is a wonderful experience for tourists to the Cook Islands, whether it's the beautiful quilts, expert weaving, or modern artwork.

Traditional Foods and Beverages

Traditional Cook Islands cuisine and beverages reflect the islands' lively Polynesian culture and wealth of fresh ingredients. Here is a list of some typical foods and drinks to try when visiting the Cook Islands:

- Ika Mata: Ika Mata is a popular traditional Cook Islands cuisine that consists of raw fish marinated in lime juice and blended with coconut cream, chopped tomatoes, onions, and sometimes chile. It's a light and flavorful meal that highlights the fresh seafood available on the islands.

- Rukau: Rukau is a traditional Cook Islands meal comprised of taro leaves cooked in coconut cream. It is often served as a side dish with other foods or as a main entrée. Rukau's creamy and somewhat earthy taste compliments a variety of meat and fish meals.

- Poke: Like its Hawaiian cousin, poke is a popular meal in the Cook Islands that consists of diced raw fish, generally tuna or yellowfin, marinated in a blend of soy sauce, sesame oil, lime juice, and seasonings. It is often served as an appetizer or light dinner and is full of fresh tastes.

- Eke: Eke is an octopus-based traditional Cook Islands meal. The octopus is often marinated in lime juice before being grilled and combined with coconut cream and other ingredients. It is then served with taro or sweet potatoes for a filling and tasty supper.

- Umu: Umu is a traditional Cook Islands cooking process, akin to Maori hangi or Hawaiian imu. Food is cooked in a subterranean oven heated by hot stones. Umu-cooked foods often feature meats such as hog, poultry, or fish, as well as vegetables and root crops, producing delicate and savory meals.

- Taro is a root vegetable popular in Cook Islands cuisine. It is often served boiled, mashed, or roasted as a side dish or as a component of other meals. Taro has a starchy texture and a somewhat nutty taste that complements a variety of traditional cuisines.

- Po'e: Po'e is a traditional Cook Islands dessert prepared from mashed ripe bananas, pumpkin, or breadfruit that is baked with coconut cream. It's a sweet and creamy pudding-like dish that's usually scented with vanilla or cinnamon and topped with a drizzle of coconut cream.

Traditional Drinks:

- Enjoy the pleasant flavor of pure coconut water direct from the source. The Cook Islands are plentiful in coconuts, and drinking their naturally delicious and hydrating water is a must-do experience.
- Bush Beer: Bush beer, also known as "matutu" or "karori," is a fermented beverage produced from the bark and roots of certain plants. It has a distinct taste and is often consumed at special occasions and cultural events.
- Noni Juice: Noni juice is made from the fruit of the noni tree, which is indigenous to the Pacific Islands. It has therapeutic characteristics and is said to offer health advantages. Noni juice comes in a variety of forms and is a favorite local beverage.

- Native Beers: Matutu Brewery and Cooks Lager are two native beer brands in the Cook Islands. Locals and tourists alike like these beers, which provide a sense of the islands.

Try these traditional foods and drinks while visiting the Cook Islands to thoroughly immerse yourself in the local culinary culture and taste the flavors of Polynesia.

Festivals & Events

The Cook Islands are noted for their vivid and exciting gatherings and festivals that display the inhabitants' rich cultural history and customs. Here are some significant events and festivals that you may attend during your visit:

- Te Maeva Nui: Te Maeva Nui is the Cook Islands' most important cultural celebration, occurring annually in July. It commemorates the islands' self-government and highlights the Cook Islands' traditional arts, music, dancing, and sports. Parades, cultural events, beauty pageants, and sports contests are all part of the celebrations.
- Tiare Festival: The Tiare Festival is a week-long celebration of the Cook Islands' national flower, the tiare maori (Gardenia taitensis). It is held in November and

includes a variety of activities such as flower shows, beauty pageants, music concerts, and cultural performances.

- Constitution Day is observed on August 4th to celebrate the establishment of the Cook Islands' constitution. Ceremonies, cultural performances, traditional activities, and feasts are held to commemorate the day.

- Anzac Day: Anzac Day is an important day of remembering in the Cook Islands, marked on April 25th. It honors the services and sacrifices made by the military forces of Australia and New Zealand. Dawn services, parades, and wreath-laying rituals are held to commemorate the day.

- Gospel Day is a religious celebration held on the first Friday of December in the Cook Islands. It comprises church services, hymn singing, traditional choirs, and gospel music performances to highlight the islands' strong Christian religion.

- Punanga Nui Market Night: The Punanga Nui Market Night is a bustling cultural event held on Saturday nights in Avarua, the capital of Rarotonga, where tourists may enjoy local food vendors, live music, and cultural performances. It's a terrific chance to immerse yourself in the vibrant environment and mingle with the people.

- Pacific Mini Games: The Cook Islands held the Pacific Mini Games in 2009, and future versions are scheduled. This multisport event invites competitors from several Pacific countries together to participate in a variety of disciplines such as athletics, rugby, swimming, and more.

Cultural nights: Many Cook Islands resorts and hotels have cultural nights that include traditional dance performances, live music, and a traditional feast called as a 'umu. These activities allow visitors to experience the islanders' lively culture and friendliness.

It's crucial to remember that event dates and timetables might change from year to year, so double-check the particular dates and information prior to your visit. Attending these events and festivals is a fantastic opportunity to immerse oneself in the Cook Islands' cultural traditions, music, dancing, and friendly hospitality.

Health and Safety Recommendations

To guarantee a seamless and pleasurable journey to the Cook Islands, it is essential to prioritize your health and safety. Here are a few health and safety reminders:

Travel Insurance: It is essential to obtain comprehensive travel insurance that covers medical bills, trip cancellations or delays, and emergency evacuations before visiting the Cook Islands. Check your insurance carefully to understand the coverage and contact details in case of an emergency.

Medical Precautions: Discuss essential immunizations and medicines with your healthcare practitioner or a travel medicine expert well in advance of your trip. Vaccines for hepatitis A and B, typhoid, tetanus, and measles, mumps, and rubella (MMR) are often recommended. It's also a good idea to have a basic medical kit with basic supplies.

Sun Protection: Because the Cook Islands have a tropical environment, it is essential to protect oneself from the harsh sun. Wear high-SPF sunscreen, protective clothes, a hat, and sunglasses. Seek shade during the warmest hours of the day and drink lots of water to keep hydrated.

Water Safety: While the Cook Islands' tap water is typically safe to drink, it is suggested that you consume bottled water or utilize water purifying procedures. While swimming in natural bodies of water, avoid swallowing water since certain regions may have powerful currents or underwater risks.

Mosquito-Borne illnesses: Although the Cook Islands are deemed low risk for mosquito-borne illnesses, measures should still be taken. Wear DEET-containing insect repellent, long-sleeved clothes and pants in the evenings, and sleep beneath mosquito netting if required.

Food & Hygiene: Maintain proper hygiene by washing your hands with soap and water before and after eating and using the toilet. Choose reputed restaurants that use good food handling and preparation standards while eating out. Avoid eating raw or undercooked seafood, as well as fruits that have been washed with tap water.

Personal Safety: The Cook Islands are typically safe for visitors, although common sense measures should be taken. Keep your valuables safe, avoid going alone at night in rural or poorly lit locations, and be aware of your surroundings. Follow the safety rules and recommendations supplied by expert guides while participating in outdoor activities.

Emergency Services: Learn the emergency contact numbers in your area, including those for medical crises, police, and fire services. Carry these numbers with you at all times, and be aware of the location of the closest medical facilities.

Respect Local Customs and Traditions: The Cook Islands have a rich cultural legacy, and it is essential to respect local customs and traditions. Learn basic manners, such as taking off your shoes before entering someone's house or a holy location.

Communication and Internet Access

Staying connected and having access to communication tools while visiting the Cook Islands may substantially improve your experience. Here are some pointers for communicating and using the internet in the Cook Islands:

Mobile Network: The Cook Islands have a dependable mobile network that covers the major islands. Bluesky Cook Islands and Digicel are the two primary mobile service providers. Both provide prepaid SIM cards that may be purchased at the airport or in local businesses. Check that your phone is unlocked and compatible with the frequencies of the local network.

Check with your mobile service provider for information on international roaming choices and charges. Roaming fees may be pricey, so it's a good idea to get a local SIM card for cheaper local calls, texts, and internet use.

Wi-Fi Access: Wi-Fi is available in most hotels, resorts, cafés, and restaurants in the Cook Islands. However, internet speed might vary, particularly in isolated regions. Before your journey, check the availability and quality of Wi-Fi with your hotel provider.

Internet Cafes: There are internet cafes on Rarotonga and Aitutaki where you may access the internet for a cost. These places provide computers with internet connection, so you can remain connected and explore the web.

Free Wi-Fi Hotspots in Public Places: Some public places, such as airports, libraries, and some cafés, may have free Wi-Fi hotspots. However, these connections may have speed and security constraints. When utilizing public Wi-Fi networks, use care and avoid accessing sensitive information or conducting financial activities.

Apps for Communication: Consider installing communication apps like WhatsApp, Skype, or Viber. Using an internet connection, you may use these applications to conduct voice and video conversations, send messages, and share photographs and videos. They might be an inexpensive method to communicate with relatives and friends back home.

Internet connectivity in distant Areas: If you visit the Cook Islands' more distant islands, be advised that internet connectivity may be restricted or non-existent. Plan ahead of time and notify your contacts of any probable communication difficulties during your trip.

When utilizing public networks or Wi-Fi hotspots, keep your mobile devices and personal information safe. On insecure networks, avoid exchanging critical information or accessing confidential accounts.

Staying connected and navigating the digital world in the Cook Islands is possible if you are prepared and use the various communication alternatives.

ATMs and banking

When visiting the Cook Islands, it is important to understand the financial system and the availability of ATMs. Here are some details about banking and ATMs in the Cook Islands:

The Cook Islands' official currency is the New Zealand dollar (NZD). The Cook Islands also have their own currency, the Cook Islands dollar (CID), which has a fixed exchange rate with the New Zealand dollar. Cook Islands money and New Zealand coins and banknotes are interchangeable.

Banking Hours: Banks in the Cook Islands are normally open from 9:00 a.m. to 3:00 p.m., Monday through Friday. On Fridays, certain banks may have shortened hours or shut for lunch. It is recommended that you verify the exact banking hours of the branch you want to visit.

ATMs: In the Cook Islands, ATMs may be found in major cities and tourist destinations, notably on the main island of Rarotonga. ATMs are linked to major worldwide networks like Visa and Mastercard, enabling you to withdraw cash with your debit or credit card. Keep in mind that some smaller islands may have limited or no ATMs, so bring adequate cash for your requirements.

Cash withdrawals: You may withdraw New Zealand dollars from ATMs in the Cook Islands. It's crucial to know that ATM transactions may be subject to costs, such as foreign withdrawal fees imposed by your bank or card issuer. Before your vacation, check with your bank to see if there are any costs or limitations.

It's also a good idea to advise your bank of your trip intentions to prevent having your card stopped for suspicious behaviour.

Money Exchange: If you need to exchange foreign money, you may do so at Cook Islands banks. cash exchange operations may be handled by major banks, although it is suggested that you convert your cash into New Zealand dollars before arriving in the Cook Islands for better prices and ease.

Credit Cards: Major credit cards like as Visa and Mastercard are frequently accepted at Cook Islands hotels, resorts, restaurants, and bigger institutions. However, carrying cash is always a smart idea for smaller stores, marketplaces, and local sellers who may not take cards.

Traveler's checks: In the Cook Islands, travelers' checks are not generally recognized. For your financial requirements, it is preferable to use cash or debit/credit cards.

Banking Services: In addition to cash withdrawals and currency exchange, banks in the Cook Islands provide account enquiries, deposits, and, in certain cases, international money transfer services. If you want specialized financial services, you should go to the major branches of the banks on Rarotonga's main island.

Keep your money and valuables safe when traveling, and tell your bank promptly if any cards are lost or stolen. In case of any unexpected events, it's also a good idea to carry a backup payment option, such as a separate card or emergency cash.

Electrical and Power Outlets

When visiting the Cook Islands, it is essential to understand the country's electrical regulations and power plugs. Here's some information regarding power outlets and energy in the Cook Islands:

Voltage: The Cook Islands have a standard voltage of 240 volts and a frequency of 50 hertz. This voltage is compatible with the majority of electrical equipment used in Australia, New Zealand, and the United Kingdom.

Power Sockets: The Cook Islands employ Type I power sockets, which are the same as those used in Australia and New Zealand. Three flat pins are placed in a diagonal line in these sockets, with the top pin being somewhat longer than the other two. It is critical to verify whether your gadgets are Type I compliant or to carry required adapters.

Adapters & Converters: If your nation uses a different style of power socket or works on a different voltage than the Cook Islands, you will need a compatible adapter or converter to use your electrical gadgets. An adapter enables you to connect your gadgets into the local power outlets, however a voltage converter is required if your electronics are not compatible with the local standard.

Adapters are readily available at most electronics shops, travel supply stores, and internet sellers prior to your journey. It is advised that you determine the sort of adapter you need depending on the power socket standard in your native country.

Chargers: If you want to charge electrical devices such as cellphones, cameras, and computers, be sure your chargers are compatible with the local voltage. Most current electrical equipment are built to tolerate a broad variety of voltages, but double-check before connecting them in.

Power Outlets: Depending on where you stay, power outlets may or may not be available. Some lodgings may offer several power outlets in their rooms, while others may have just a few. If you have many gadgets that need to be charged at the same time, bring a power strip or a multi-socket extension cable.

Power Outages: The Cook Islands, like many other tropical places, may have power outages or disruptions from time to time. In the event of a power outage, it's a good idea to carry a portable power bank or backup batteries for your important gadgets, such as cellphones.

You can guarantee that you have the right power source to keep your gadgets charged and running throughout your stay in the Cook Islands by being prepared with the appropriate adapters and considering the voltage needs of your electrical equipment.

Etiquette and Tipping

It's important to learn local norms and practices when it comes to tipping and etiquette in the Cook Islands. Here are some pointers to assist you with tipping and manners throughout your visit:

Tipping is not often anticipated or performed in the Cook Islands. However, because to the impact of foreign tourists, it is becoming increasingly widespread in tourist locations. A little tip is optional if you get great service or desire to express your thanks.

Restaurants and Bars: Some premium restaurants and resorts may include a service fee in the bill, removing the need for extra tipping. If there is no service charge, a little tip of roughly 10% is appropriate if you believe the service was good. Tipping is rarely customary in smaller, local restaurants or informal eating locations.

Similarly, tipping is not commonly anticipated in Cook Islands hotels, resorts, or guesthouses. However, if you experience extraordinary treatment from a member of the staff, such as cleaning or the concierge, you may leave a modest tip as a token of your gratitude.

Tour Guides and Drivers: Tipping is not required but appreciated if you engage in guided tours or utilize transportation services with a driver. Consider tipping drivers that give outstanding service or go above and beyond for 5-10% of the tour fee or a modest amount.

Tipping taxi drivers is not customary in the Cook Islands. Typically, fare costs are predetermined, and rounding up to the closest dollar suffices. However, if a driver delivers great service or aids with baggage, you may leave a little tip as a thank you.

Cultural Sensitivity: In terms of etiquette, it is essential to respect the Cook Islands' indigenous culture and traditions. When visiting communities or attending traditional rites, dress modestly. Before entering houses or holy locations, remove your shoes and get permission before photographing individuals or cultural objects.

Polite welcomes: The Cook Islands have a welcoming culture, and welcomes are an integral aspect of everyday life. When greeting natives, it is usual to exchange a cordial "Kia Orana" (which means "hello" or "may you live long"). Accept the welcoming environment and return the nice gestures.

While tipping is not a major cultural standard in the Cook Islands, expressing thanks and appreciation for excellent service is always appreciated. It is essential to be polite and follow local traditions in order to create a good and pleasurable experience for both tourists and residents.

Customs and Local Laws

To guarantee a respectful and pleasurable stay in the Cook Islands, it is vital to get acquainted with the local laws and traditions. Here are some important facts about Cook Islands laws and customs:

Respect for Culture: The Cook Islands have a vibrant Polynesian culture, and it is essential to respect their traditions and practices. Locals value tourists who are interested in their culture, so be open-minded and eager to learn.

Traditional procedures: Traditional procedures and customs are still observed in the Cook Islands. It is vital to request permission before attending a marae (holy gathering place) and to respect any unique traditions or rituals that may be going place.

Dress Code: It is polite to dress modestly while visiting villages or attending cultural activities. When visiting traditional settings or residences, avoid wearing exposing apparel, especially for ladies, and remove caps and sunglasses.

Public Behaviour: It is important to act politely in public places. Avoid being loud or disturbing, particularly in residential settings. Except in authorized settings, drinking alcohol in public places is normally illegal.

The Cook Islands are noted for their beautiful natural surroundings. It is critical to respect and conserve the ecosystems of the islands by not littering, avoiding harm to coral reefs and marine life when snorkeling or diving, and following any conservation rules that are presented.

Drug Laws: Illegal drug possession and usage are highly forbidden in the Cook Islands. This includes marijuana, which is outlawed in the United States while being lawful in certain other nations or states. Violations may result in harsh penalties, including imprisonment.

Driving restrictions: If you want to drive in the Cook Islands, get acquainted with the local driving rules and restrictions. Keep in mind to drive on the left side of the road, use seat belts, and obey speed restrictions. Driving while intoxicated is definitely forbidden.

Photography and Privacy: Always get permission before photographing anyone, particularly when photographing locals, cultural activities, or holy locations. Respect their privacy and be sensitive to cultural differences.

Wildlife and conservation: The Cook Islands feature distinct and vulnerable ecosystems. It is critical to preserve the environment and obey animal protection standards, which include marine life and bird sanctuaries. Touching or disturbing animals is prohibited, as is collecting or removing natural resources such as shells or coral.

Same-Sex partnerships: Although same-sex partnerships are allowed in the Cook Islands, public demonstrations of love may be less usual than in more progressive places. It is vital to be aware of local traditions and cultural sensitivities.

Before traveling to the Cook Islands, it is usually a good idea to study and learn the local laws and traditions. This will assist to guarantee that you have a courteous and pleasurable visit while also positively contributing to the local community and environment.

Money Saving Tips in Cook Islands

The Cook Islands, like other Pacific islands, are not the cheapest location to visit – but they are far less expensive than other places in the area. If you're searching for ways to save money while visiting, here are some ideas:

Bike around the islands instead than using cabs! Bike rentals cost roughly 20-30 NZD per day, however multi-day rentals may be as little as 13-15 NZD per day. It's an inexpensive and enjoyable way to travel.

Eat the local cuisine - A full plate of native cuisine costs roughly 6 NZD if you stick to small, traditional places rather than resorts and large tourist locations.

Shop duty-free - If you intend on consuming wine or strong alcohol, purchase it ahead of time at duty-free rather than on the island. Beer is reasonably priced, but most other alcoholic beverages are not.

Stay with a local - If you prepare ahead, you should be able to locate a Couchsurfing host (albeit there aren't many in the Cook Islands). This way, you not only have a place to stay, but you may also meet a local who can give insider information.

Save money on inter-island flights - Domestic flights between the islands are outrageously costly, but if you show up to the Air Rarotonga office to book a last-minute ticket, you may be able to secure a significant discount.

Use hotel points - If you really want to splurge, cash in your travel hacking points and stay at a resort. Having free lodging can significantly reduce your expenditures! Here's how to start earning free flights and hotels now!

Pack a water bottle - Because the tap water in this area is typically regarded as safe, you may skip the bottled water. You'll save money and reduce your consumption of single-use plastic. To be safe, having a reusable water bottle with a filter is a smart idea. LifeStraw is my favored bottle since it features a built-in filter that ensures your water is always pure and safe.

Itinerary for 3 Days:

Day 1:

Morning:

Arrive at Rarotonga and check into your hotel.

Explore the Muri Lagoon, go swimming, and relax on the beautiful beach.

Afternoon:

Te Vara Nui Village offers a cultural experience that includes a traditional dance display and meal.

Explore Avarua's local markets for one-of-a-kind gifts.

Evening:

Spend a quiet evening at a small restaurant sampling authentic Cook Islands food.

Day 2:

Morning:

Hike to Te Rua Manga (The Needle) in the early morning for stunning panoramic views of Rarotonga.

Learn about the history and culture of the Cook Islands at the Cook Islands National Museum in Avarua.

Afternoon:

Titikaveka Beach is a lovely place to unwind and soak up the sun.

Discover the abundant marine life by snorkeling or diving in the crystal-clear seas.

Evening:

Experience the splendor of the Cook Islands' coastline on a sunset or dinner cruise.

Day 3:

Morning:

Take a leisurely trip to Aitutaki, which is noted for its beautiful lagoon.

Discover the Aitutaki Lagoon's gorgeous beaches and coral reefs by boat or kayak.

Afternoon:

Visit One Foot Island and enjoy a beach picnic meal.

Relax and enjoy swimming in the lagoon's turquoise waters.

Evening:

Experience a "umu," a traditional Cook Islands feast in which food is cooked in an underground oven.

Enjoy an evening of live music and dance performances by local artists.

Itinerary for 7 Days:

Rarotonga on Day One

Morning:

Explore the Rarotonga Punanga Nui Market and try some of the island's fresh vegetables and crafts.

Discover the island's gorgeous jungle and learn about the native plants and wildlife on the Pa's Nature Walk.

Afternoon:

Explore the underwater world of Muri Lagoon on a snorkeling or diving adventure.

Relax and enjoy the sun at the beach.

Evening:

At one of the waterfront restaurants, enjoy a sunset supper.

Rarotonga on Day 2

Morning:

Take the Ara Tapu Road around the island, pausing at views and secluded beaches.

Visit the Maire Nui Gardens, a lovely botanical park with an array of tropical species.

Afternoon:

Take a guided climb up the Cross Island Track and appreciate the summit's magnificent views.

Discover Takitumu Conservation Area's historical sites.

Evening:

Experience traditional music, dancing, and storytelling by attending a cultural performance.

Aitutaki on the third day

Morning:

Take an early morning flight to Aitutaki and settle into your hotel.

Explore the beautiful Aitutaki Lagoon by boat or kayak, stopping at several motus (islets).

Afternoon:

Spend the day swimming, snorkeling, and relaxing on One Foot Island following a picnic lunch.

Evening:

Enjoy supper aboard a sunset sail in the lagoon.

Day Four: Aitutaki

Morning:

Go on a fishing trip and try your luck at capturing some local fish.

Learn about the local culture and customs by visiting Arutanga Village.

Afternoon:

Discover the historical importance of the Cook Islands by visiting the ancient marae at Arai Te Tonga.

Local artists create traditional items at Ee Island items.

Evening:

Immerse yourself in Cook Islands cuisine by partaking in a traditional umu feast.

Atiu, Day 5

Morning:

Fly to Atiu, which is recognized for its distinctive limestone caverns and unspoilt natural beauty.

Explore the beautiful rock formations of Anatakitaki Cave.

Afternoon:

Visit local communities and learn about the island's unique practices on a guided tour of Atiu.

Explore the Makatea Cliffs and take in the breathtaking views.

Evening:

Enjoy a typical Atiu island night complete with indigenous music, dancing, and a feast.

Day Six: Atiu

Morning:

Discover the abundant birds and lush woodlands of Atiu on a guided nature walk.

Learn about the local customs and traditions by visiting the Tumunu (traditional gathering place).

Afternoon:

Swimming and snorkeling are popular activities on Atiu's gorgeous beaches.

Explore the Tiroto Tunnel, a spectacular stalactite creation in an old cave system.

Evening:

On the beach, enjoy a sunset meal.

Rarotonga on Day 7

Morning:

Return to Rarotonga and relax on the beach for the morning.

Visit Black Rock Beach to see the ancient ritual of "jumping off the rock."

Afternoon:

Unwind and relax with a spa treatment or a classic massage.

For one-of-a-kind gifts, visit the local art galleries and boutiques.

Evening:

Enjoy a goodbye supper at a local restaurant and reminisce on your fantastic Cook Islands adventure.

Remember to customize the itineraries depending on your tastes and the exact places and activities you want to do. The Cook Islands have a wide variety of activities to offer, and these itineraries seek to give a balanced combination of cultural immersion, outdoor excursions, relaxation, and discovery.

CHAPTER 7: Additional Resources

Websites and Online Guides

There are various websites and online guides that may give helpful information and tools while arranging a vacation to the Cook Islands. Here are some websites and online guides that may be of use to you:

Cook Islands tourist Official Website (www.cookislands.travel): The Cook Islands' official tourist website gives detailed information on the islands, including lodging alternatives, activities, attractions, and travel advice. It also has a useful travel planning function.

Cook Islands News (www.cookislandsnews.com): This is the Cook Islands' major news source, providing information on current events, local news, and cultural activities. It might be a helpful tool for staying up to speed on the latest developments and activities throughout your visit.

Cook Islands Herald (www.ciherald.co.ck): The Cook Islands Herald is another news newspaper in the Cook Islands that covers local news, events, and cultural features of the islands. It gives insights into the community as well as information on a variety of issues of interest.

Journey Era's Cook Islands Travel Guide (www.journeyera.com): Journey Era's online travel guide gives thorough information about the Cook Islands, including suggestions, itineraries, and activity and attraction recommendations. It shares the author's own ideas and experiences from his trips in the area.

These websites and online guides might be helpful when researching and organizing a trip to the Cook Islands. They provide a lot of information about lodgings, activities, and destinations, as well as practical travel advice to help you make the most of your stay.

Useful Apps and Tools for Users

There are various handy applications and tools available in today's digital age that may improve your Cook Islands vacation experience. Here are some programs and tools to think about:

Cook Islands Travel reference App: This app offers a thorough reference to the Cook Islands, including information on sights, lodging, food, and activities. It includes offline maps, travel recommendations, and the option to construct custom itineraries.

Google Maps: This popular navigation program can help you travel around the Cook Islands. It offers precise maps, instructions, and real-time traffic updates. You may also store offline maps to use when you don't have access to the internet.

Currency Converter: When dealing with multiple currencies in the Cook Islands, an app that enables you to convert currencies might come in helpful. It allows you to swiftly compute prices and determine the worth of your money.

Weather Apps: It is important to keep an eye on the weather while planning outdoor activities in the Cook Islands. AccuWeather, Weather.com, and the MetService app (local weather service) can give reliable weather predictions to assist you in planning your days.

Cook Islands Maori Language App: If you want to learn a few Cook Islands Maori phrases, there are language applications that can aid you with pronunciation, vocabulary, and fundamental phrases.

TripIt: This trip organizing tool keeps track of your itinerary, flights, lodging, and other travel data. It centralizes all of your trip information in one location, making it simple to access and share with others.

XE Currency: This app offers real-time currency conversion and exchange rates. It might be beneficial for rapidly verifying the value of the local currency and ensuring you understand pricing and costs.

Cook Islands Radio: Listen to Cook Islands radio stations through specific applications or internet platforms and immerse yourself in the local culture. During your stay, you may listen to local music, read the news, and see cultural programs.

Remember to download and install these applications before to your travel to ensure you have offline access and that they are tailored to your preferences. While these applications and tools may improve your trip experience, it's always a good idea to have a backup plan in case of technology troubles or restricted internet access, such as packing paper maps or guidebooks.

CONCLUSION

Finally, the Cook Islands are a wonderfully intriguing location with a wealth of natural beauty, unique cultural experiences, and kind friendliness. This thorough travel guide has given you a lot of information to help you plan and maximize your vacation to the Cook Islands. The Cook Islands provide something for every sort of tourist, from the gorgeous beaches and crystal-clear oceans to the lively culture and broad choice of activities. This Pacific paradise offers rest, action, or a combination of the two.

We began with an overview of the Cook Islands, delving into its history, culture, and traditions. Understanding and appreciating the local way of life is vital for an enjoyable experience. We next went through the practical components of preparing your trip, such as visa requirements, important information to know, safety and security precautions, and communication choices.

When visiting the Cook Islands, time is everything. We reviewed the optimum time to visit, taking into account things such as weather, people, and special events. In addition, we advised you on the length of your stay, assisting you in deciding how long to spend on this island paradise.

Getting to the Cook Islands is made simpler with information on flights, airport transportation, and several ways to get about the islands. We discussed public transit, vehicle rentals, bicycles, scooters, and even the magnificent walking and hiking paths that are accessible for those who prefer a more active tour.

lodgings ranged from resorts and hotels to guesthouses, bed and breakfasts, self-catering lodgings, and even camping and hiking possibilities. For a smooth and comfortable visit, we gave insights on the best neighborhoods to stay as well as areas to avoid.

We provided a variety of activities and attractions to help you make the most of your stay in the Cook Islands. There is much to see and do, from beach and ocean sports to cultural experiences, outdoor excursions, historical monuments, shopping, cuisine, and nightlife. The book also emphasized the importance of dancing and music, art and crafts, traditional meals and beverages, and exciting events and festivals held throughout the year.

We discussed topics such as health and safety, communication and internet access, banking and ATMs, electricity and power sockets, tipping and etiquette, local laws and customs, language and useful phrases, and how to navigate the islands with ease and respect for the local culture.

To summarize, the Cook Islands are a location that combines natural beauty, cultural depth, and genuine friendliness. You'll be well-equipped to plan your vacation, make educated choices, and create wonderful experiences in this gorgeous South Pacific paradise if you use our thorough travel guide. So pack your bags, dive into the turquoise seas, enjoy the lively culture, and prepare to be enchanted by the Cook Islands.

Printed in Great Britain
by Amazon

25095391R00086